20-

An English photographer in Rome
ROBERT MACPHERSON

The authors are particularly grateful to Mario Becchetti for his kind assistance, especially in tracking down rare and little-known texts. We would also like to thank the following individuals and organisations for permission to publish photographs from their collections: Lucia Cavazzi, Director of the Municipal Photographic Archives in Rome; Rossella Ruggeri, Director of the Luigi Poletti Library in Modena; Christie's in South Kensington, London; Gianfranco Desantis in Rome; the Martini and Ronchetti Gallery in Genoa; Erich Sommer in London and the Texbraun Gallery in Paris.
Finally, the authors wish to express their sincere gratitude to the collector who, wishing to remain anonymous, has allowed the publication of the majority of the photographs in this book.

English translation by Elspeth Thompson

Copyright 1988 Rome – Edizioni Quasar di Severino Tognon
Via Quattro Novembre 152 – 00187 Roma – tel. 6789888

ISBN 88-85020-87-9

PIERO BECCHETTI - CARLO PIETRANGELI

An English photographer in Rome
ROBERT MACPHERSON

EDIZIONI QUASAR

CONTENTS

ROME AT THE TIME OF PIUS IX

THE METAMORPHOSIS OF ROME

Robert Macpherson's work as a photographer spanned the reign of Pope Pius IX, and he remains one of the most sensitive and observant interpreters of the Rome of that time. It would seem best to begin an appraisal of his work with an attempt to build up a mental picture of the Rome handed down to us through his photographs.

These notes have been restricted to the reign of Pius IX because, from 1870 onwards, the face of the city began to undergo a remarkable change as a result of the vast range of public works either completed or underway by that date. And even between 1846 and 1870, in spite of all the difficulties created by political events, a whole series of developments sprang up which, though they may not have had such a profound impact on the appearance of the city as a whole, still brought some distinct and not always fortunate changes in their wake.

Pius IX's architects

The principal architects involved in work on the buildings, monuments and town planning at this time were: Luigi Poletti (1792-1869), Luigi Canina (1795-1856), Antonio Sarti (1797-1881), Virginio Vespignani (1808-1882), Andrea Busiri Vici (1818-1911), Salvatore Bianchi (1821-1884), Antonio Cipolla (1823-1874) and Francesco Azzurri (1831-1901). We have left out the less important names whose influence was mainly on private architecture, rather than on the city's monuments and public works.

Restoration of Roman churches

An ambitious campaign to restore and embellish Rome's churches was launched during the reign of Pius IX.

Starting with the major basilicas, this included the placing of the two colossal statues of St. Peter and St. Paul in front of St. Peter's (1847) and the construction of the new house for the Beneficianti next to the Marchioni Sacristy (1863-4). The rebuilding of St. Peter's after the fire of 1823 continued with zeal; the basilica was reconsecrated in 1854 and the adjoining campanile by Poletti was erected in 1860. At S. Giovanni the confessional and papal altar were renovated, and there was already talk of the need to enlarge the presbytery – this was done later under Leo XIII. The nearby sixteenth century sanctuary of the Scala Sancta underwent some rather unwise alterations and the new convent of the Passionisti was built next door (1854). At S. Maria Maggiore the new confessional was installed.

Very few of Rome's churches escaped the Pope's restorative zeal, and many ancient and precious buildings which had been preserved almost intact up to that time were irrevocably altered. A few of the many are listed below in chronological order.

The interiors of S. Anastasia and S. Pancrazio were restored in 1850, while at S. Maria in Monserrato the decorations were restored and the adjoining Spanish College was built (1851-62). A variety of restoration work was carried out at SS. Vincenzo e Anastasia alle Tre Fontane (1852); part of the monastery of S. Marta was rebuilt (1852); the interior of SS. Bonifacio e Alessio was renovated (1852-60) and a major restoration project carried out at Spirito Santo dei Napoletani by

Angiolini and Tuminello, Portrait of Pius IX, around 1873. (Coll. P. Becchetti, Rome).

Ferdinand II, King of the Two Sicilies, in 1853. At S. Agnese *extra moenia* the interior was renovated and the monastery of the Canonici Regolari Lateranesi was built (1855-56). Various works were carried out at S. Agnese in Piazza Navona (1855-64), at S. Spirito in Sassia (1856), at S. Onofrio (the chapel containing the tomb of Tasso, 1857), at S. Bernardo (1857), S. Lorenzo in Lucina (1857-58), S. Carlo ai Catinari (1857-61) and SS. Nome di Maria (1857-67). S. Bernardo alle Terme (1858), S. Ivo (1859), S. Vitale (1859), S. Croce and S. Bonaventura dei Lucchesi (1859-63), S. Lucia del Gonfalone (1859-67) and S. Maria in Monticelli (1860) all underwent repairs, while the Natività in Piazza Pasquino was given a new facade in 1861 and S. Maria in Aquiro and S. Marcello were restored between 1861 and 1867. The chapel of S. Paolo della Croce at SS. Giovanni e Paolo was completed in 1862, and internal works and a new facade were finished at S. Salvatore in Lauro in 1862. Work was also carried out at S. Maria in Via Lata (1862-63), S. Lorenzo fuori le Mura (1862-65; the column in front of the basilica was set up in 1865), at S. Giacomo in Augusta (1863), S. Rocco (completed in 1864) and S. Giovanni Battista dei Genovesi (restored between 1864-76, with the new facade dating from 1864). The following churches were also restored: S. Nicola in Carcere (1865), the confessional at S. Francesca Romana (1866-69), S. Maria in Trastevere (1866-74), S. Tommaso di Canterbury (completely rebuilt in 1866-88), SS. Celso e Giuliano in Banchi (work completed in 1868), S. Agostino (finished in 1868), S. Lorenzo in Damaso (1868-82), S. Andrea della Valle (Chapel of S. Sebastiano, 1869), S. Angelo in Peschieria (1869-70), S. Antonio dei Portoghesi (completed in 1870) and S. Pudenziana (1870).

The list could go on even longer. Few new churches were built during this period – only the Madonna dell'Archetto (1851), S. Maria del Carmine and S. Giuseppe fuori Porta Portese (1854) and S. Alfonso de' Liguori (1859). But other new religious buildings included the new oratory in the Casa Professa of the Jesuits (1861), the Scottish College (1864), the Polish College near S. Adriano (completed in 1866), the Latin American College in Piazza della Minerva (1862-71) and the North American College in Via dell'Umiltà (1866). The Pius V chapel in the grounds of the Scuole Notturne di Religione outside Porta Cavalleggeri was constructed in 1853, the Pius Seminary in Piazza S. Apollinare in 1853-54 and the Borromeo Conservatory in Via Graziosa in 1864.

The column in Piazza di Spagna was erected in 1855-57 to mark the final definition of the dogma of the Immaculate Conception of Mary in 1854, and in 1848 a shrine was built outside Porta S. Pancrazio to celebrate the discovery of the head of St. Andrew.

The Quirinal and the Vatican

Some important restoration work was carried out to the Papal Palace on the Quirinal and its surroundings (Palazzo della Dataria 1860-61; Palazzo di S. Felice 1864-64) and, of course, in the Vatican. Here, Martinucci built the new steps into the S. Damasco courtyard which finished with a low portico to one side of St. Peter's.

Cultural activities

Noteworthy efforts to preserve the ancient monuments were made at this time – witnessed by the restoration of the Colosseum and the Pantheon, the excavation of the Basilica Julia and the reconstruction of the Porticus of the Dei Consenti. Excavations were carried out on the Palatine, the colossal bronze statue of Hercules was discovered near Campo dei Fiori (1864) and the Apoxyomenos of Lysippos unearthed in Trastevere (1849). Other excavations cleared and consolidated the remains of the three temples of S. Nicola in Carcere, the structures beneath the church of S. Anastasia and the Mithraeum under the secondary basilica of S. Clemente (1867). The excubitorium of the Seventh Cohort of the Vigiles was discovered in Trastevere in 1867, the basilica of S. Stefano and the tombs of the Via Latina were cleared in 1857-58, and the Via Appia was restored in 1852. Excavations were also made at the Tiber emporium and the Villa of Livia at

Prima Porta, where the famous statue of Augustus was found in 1863. Many discoveries were also made in the Catacombs.

The Papal projects extended to museums. A new Gallery of Saints and the Blessed was created in the Vatican Museums to house paintings commemorating canonisations and beatifications, and improvements were carried out to the Library. In the Lateran, the Pio-Cristiano Museum was added to the Museo Profano and the picture gallery. Astronomical observatories were built on the Capitoline Hill and in the Collegio Romano in 1853, and at the latter, the university museums of human anatomy, geology, minerology and physics were established. The Botanic Gardens, which were then behind the Palazzo Salviati, were equipped with new greenhouses, and the Palazzo Camerale di Ripetta, constructed by Pietro Camporese the younger in 1847, became the Academy of Fine Arts.

As regards Rome's theatres, the Alibert and the Tor di Nona were restored in 1859 and 1862.

Hospitals, charitable and educational institutions

Work was also carried out in the hospitals: at S. Giovanni Calibita (an obstetrics clinic), at S. Spirito (an anatomical laboratory, new ward, and cloister and chapel for the Capuchins in 1856) and at S. Giacomo (a women's ward). The S. Maria della Pietà mental hospital was established in the Lungara near Porta S. Spirito and in 1854 a new wing for women was added to the Buon Pastore prison.

At the Verano Cemetery the vast courtyard, the church (1860-61) and the new monumental entrance (1870) were erected.

A home for the deaf and dumb was opened in 1858 near the Baths of Diocletian, where the Grand Hotel now stands. Busiri designed a boys' school in Piazza Pia (1859) and others for girls were founded on the Caelian (1867), in the Borgo Vittorio (1859) and at Monte Mario (1858). Many religious 'night' schools were also established. A boarding school was set up in the monastery of the Bambin Gesù in 1857 and, lastly, the Istituto Agrario di Carità was founded at Vigna Pia on the Via Portuense.

The city's defences

The city walls were badly in need of repair after the siege of 1849. Extensive work was done on the Janiculum and the Pincian, while the Porta S. Pancrazio and the outer face of the Porta Pia were completely restored in 1856 and 1864.

New military barracks were erected in the Castro Pretorio (1862-64), and an artillery arsenal, a riding school and a depot for wagon trains were installed in the Vatican.

Access to the other bank of the Tiber was improved by the construction of the iron walkway on the Ponte Senatorio (1853) and the suspension bridge at S. Giovanni dei Fiorentini (1863). Ponte Milvio, which had been damaged in the fighting of 1849, was also restored.

The urban layout

Trastevere was transformed between 1860 and 1865, when the Tobacco Factory was built. All the surrounding area was rearranged according to a unifying masterplan which included a wide throughfare, leading off the Stradone di S. Francesco a Ripa through Busiri's two great propylaea (1863), and ending up in a piazza with a fountain in front of the tobacco factory. Other works were planned in this area (including the Palazzo delle Scuole Cristiane, the Palazzo delle Scuole Notturne and the Collegio Apostolico delle Missioni Straniere).

Several other changes to the urban layout were completed in this period. The Piazza del Quirinale was altered by Vespignani in 1866; the Piazza Pia, giving access to the Borghi, was refashioned in 1861, with two new buildings at the top end on either side and a fountain in the centre (by Martinucci in 1862). Minor changes were made in the Via Piè di Marmo (1852), the Promenade on the Pincian was completed, and from what is now Via Garibaldi, a new route up to the Janiculum was created (1867).

New technology and its impact on Rome

Under Pius IX Rome acquired its first railway, with the stations of Porta Maggiore (1856), Porta Portese (1859) and Termini (1867-74), and the new swing bridge for the Rome-Civitavecchia line, which was constructed in 1863. The use of gas lighting spread rapidly during this period and the gasworks at the Circus Maximus date from 1853. The Acqua Marcia aqueduct was restored and renamed the Pia (1865-70) and its mostra was built where the Dogali obelisk (1870) now stands. The telegraph system entered into operation and in 1862 a head offices was installed in the Palazzo del Vicegerente (Wedekind) in Piazza Montecitorio, while the post offices were set up in Palazzo Madama.

Popular housing projects went ahead in Trastevere and near S. Clemente (1862), and public lavatories were constructed in various parts of the city (such as S. Clemente and S. Onofrio).

In 1850 the city had a population of 170,824; by 1870 this had grown to about 226,000. People travelled around mainly on foot, or else in carriages, and there was also a public carriage service. The first horse-drawn 'omnibuses' appeared in 1866; one route connected the Piazza del Popolo with the Piazza Venezia; another continued on to St Peter's.

During the Napoleonic era the streets had been lit by oil lamps. These were later replaced by petroleum lamps, and from 1854 gas lamps were installed in many areas. By 1870 there were 2000 gas lanterns, but many of the old petroleum ones continued to function. Every night the 'accenditori' or lamplighters would make the rounds of the city, lighting up the lanterns. Moonlight was taken into consideration, with a shorter period of illumination whenever there was a full moon.

Private buildings

Private enterprise also had a part in the renovation of Rome. With the Public Building and Ornamentation Regulations of 1864, many residential districts were renovated, among them the areas around the Piazza di Spagna and the Piazza del Popolo.

The works undertaken during the reign of Pius IX are illustrated in three volumes of large lithographic plates, published by Paolo Cacchiatelli and Gregorio Cleter in 1865 (second edition). As well as paintings and prints, other well-known documentation of the period includes the photographs by Altobelli, the Dovizielli, Cuccioni, Tuminello and those commissioned by Parker – and we must not forget the still unpublished series of panoramas painted by Filippo Cretoni on the cabinets in the Vatican Library. For the development of the city, another important reference is the Census of 1866.

Rome before and after 1870

Emphasis has been placed on the works completed under Pius IX to bring home the point that the Rome which was handed over to the Italians in 1870 was no longer the city of the Middle Ages, the Renaissance or even the Baroque era. It was an urban centre which was already in the process of change and development, although retaining its picturesque character to an extraordinary degree – mainly due to the striking contrasts between the monumental and the ramshackle aspects of the city. These were highlighted by Ippolito Taine in 1864, who described Rome as 'a provincial city, badly kept, badly laid out, Baroque and filthy, with narrow muddy streets filled with hovels and sheds and washing strung out to dry, and a multitude of grand buildings with enormous gratings on the windows, crossed bars and bolts, which give the impression of a fortress or a prison.'

1870 brought a clean break with the past. In fact, when the Italians entered the city through the breach at Porta Pia, one chapter of Roman history ended and another began. With this event the beloved dream city of poets and travellers, which still nestled within its walls, hardly touched by the germs of progress which had infected other cities, changed its appearance almost overnight. Its new function as capital of a young state meant that not only new buildings but also a whole new ethos was needed – and one very different from that now associated with the unpopular regime of the past.

This led first of all to the conversion of convents and monasteries into public offices and the construction of houses for the officials and their families who had been transferred to Rome. Only then could the gradual re-moulding of the face of the city begin, aided by a host of new planning regulations.

Ferdinando Gregorius' *Roman Journal* of 1871 gives a good idea of the revolution brought about in Rome by the new political situation: 'Rome has been transformed into a whitened tomb. All the houses have been whitened – even the most stately ancient palaces – and only now that the rust of centuries has been scraped away can one see just how ugly much of Rome's architecture really is. Rosa has even given the Colosseum a shave – that is to say he has freed it from all the plants and weeds that used to adorn it so well. In the process he has completely destroyed the *flora* of the Colosseum, about which an Englishman called Deakin wrote a whole book some years ago. The metamorphosis of this holy city into a temporal state is the reverse of the earlier but similarly zealous transformation of pagan Rome into Christian Rome. Convents are changed into offices; old windows are unblocked and new windows and doors created. After centuries of darkness, sun and air penetrate once more into the closed cells of monks and nuns. In a short time, San Silvestro, the monasteries of the Filippini, of Minerva, of the Agostiniani in Campo Marzio and of the Santi Apostoli, have all been forcibly transformed in this way. The monks still living there are being driven out like badgers. It is a sad sight to see them wandering like ghosts among their old cells, cloisters and corridors. The old Rome is fading away. In twenty years time it will be a new world. I am happy, however, to have lived for so long in the old Rome.'

A WALK AROUND THE CITY

We would now like to go on a rapid tour of the city's most characteristic and significant landmarks.

The walls

The walls were still intact in 1870 and also functioned as a customs barrier. As already described, the various stretches damaged by the siege of 1849 had been repaired by Poletti, and the Porta S. Pancrazio and the outer face of the Porta Pia had been completely rebuilt by Vespignani.

In 1870 the Porta Salaria was seriously damaged by artillery fire. Still flanked at this time by the two semicircular towers by Aurelian, it had to be completely demolished and rebuilt. It was during this work that the monument to the young poet Quintus Sulpicius Maximus was discovered. The Porta Pinciana was still walled up and the Porta Flaminia consisted of only one passageway with two side towers built by Sixtus IV. These were demolished in 1877 to open up the two lateral passages.

Most of the other gates were more or less as they look now. The Porta Latina and the Porta Metronia, however, were closed, the Porta Maggiore had been repaired some years before by

Gregory XIV and the picturesque Porta Tiburtina, with its double gates still in operation, had survived until 1869. In the Leonine City, only the Porta Angelica, from Pius IV's time, and the fifteenth century Porta Cavalleggeri were open – both have since been demolished.

The gates still had their huge wooden gateposts, and were guarded by customs officers. The small eighteenth century customs house at Porta S. Paolo is still standing, while the corresponding one at Porta S. Lorenzo has been demolished. The photographs of the period, particularly the Parker series, record some of the most unusual and attractive features of the walls, such as the wooden fences around the recesses by the towers, where it was possible to take refuge while herds of oxen passed by.

The course of the Tiber

The Tiber used to run between houses built out over the water, past gardens, flowering terraces and small beaches overflowing with plants. The riverside was enlivened by landing stages, floating flour mills and fishing poles or 'giornelli', which rotated with the current to catch fish. Only at Castel S. Angelo did harsh fortifications drop down sheer to the river.

Many bridges crossed the river – Ponte S. Angelo, with its three arches, the aged Ponte Sisto, with its elegant Renaissance hog-backed design, now spoilt by the iron footbridge superimposed on it in 1877, and the two ancient Roman bridges to the Tiber Island, one of which was reconstructed using the original materials in 1892. Under Pius IX two more bridges had been added: one made out of metal girders which put the Ponte Rotta back into operation, and the other a completely new iron construction at S. Giovanni ai Fiorentini.

Downstream from the town, a drawbridge had been built for the Pio-Centrale railway which had been extended from Porta Portese station up to Termini. Three ferry boats were in operation: one at Ripetta, one behind S. Biagio della Pagnotta and the third at Via della Barchetta, which took its name from the ferry.

Ripetta and Ripagrande were then the only river ports in Rome. The first, an exquisite eighteenth century panorama by Alessandro Specchi, was to be the most renowned victim of the later embankment project. It was used by the longboats with their cargos of wine, oil, coal and wood which came down from Umbria and Sabina, and from 1842 onwards, became the starting point for a regular service of steamboats going upstream to Ponte Felice (which is now destroyed but used to be near the Borghetto di Civita Castellana).

Ripagrande was a real port with a lighthouse, warehouses, customs house and arsenal where the steamboats used to arrive from Fiumicino.

After the disastrous floods of 1870 the floating mills disappeared and the river began a gradual change which culminated in the construction of the embankment between 1876 and 1900. A series of photographs records the banks before the havoc began. We can try to follow the course of the Tiber at that time, bearing in mind the fact that most of the buildings mentioned are no longer in existence.

Beginning with the left bank, after the slaughter houses and the Campo Boario (near the present day Piazzale Flaminio) and the tree-lined Passeggiata di Ripetta (all that remained of the 'quais' planned by the French administration in the early 1800s), the Academy of Fine Arts looked out over the river.

Next came the Port of Ripetta, centred around S. Girolamo degli Schiavoni and crowned by the Clement XI fountain, which also served as a lighthouse. The customs house was on the left. The river then flowed past the Collegio Clementino, the Palazzo De Romanis, the Palazzo dei Caetani all'Orso, the Church of S. Maria in Posterula (which had been handed over to the Redentoristi), and the Apollo Theatre, before arriving at Ponte S. Angelo. Immediately after the bridge was the Palazzo Altoviti with its beautiful Renaissance loggia; along this stretch were the apse of S. Giovanni dei Fiorentini, the *loggetta* (small arcade) of the Palazzo Sacchetti, the *tribuna* of S. Anna dei Bresciani and, near the Ponte Sisto, the Hospice of the Cento Preti with its fountain, backing on to the Via Giulia. After the demolished church of SS. Vincenzo e Anastasio dei Cuochi, the river passed by the Ghetto, where the houses along Via della Fiumara faced onto the water in picturesque disorder. And finally it arrived at the Foro Boario, the slopes of the Aventine, the Via Marmorata and the Emporio, where the recent excavations under Pius IX had brought to light the ancient wharves and remarkable quantities of coloured marbles.

On the right bank, after the Villa Altoviti (bought by Mons. De Merode and where the quarter of the city between the Via Vittoria Colonna, the Piazza Cavour and Castel S. Angelo would be developed), came the Castle, with its imposing fortifications. One wing of the Hospital of S. Spirito, built by Fuga and now demolished, looked out over the river, while the garden of the Farnesina and its *loggetta* (destroyed in 1884-6), also stretched down to the water.

Beyond the large wooden building of the Politeama Romano (1862-83), the river ran on towards the Tiber Island with its bridges and floating mills, to the Ponte Rotto (which still had three arches and the Church of S. Salvatore *de Pede Pontis* at the Trastevere end). It then passed the gardens of the Pamphilj at S. Maria in Cappella and the demolished *loggetta* of Donna Olimpia, and finally arrived at the Port of Ripagrande, with its lighthouse and seventeenth century porticoed customs house near Porta Portese.

The Via del Corso

Entering the city through Porta del Popolo one could head for Piazza di Spagna, or down to Piazza Venezia, or to St Peter's by following the river (or rather, the row of buildings overlooking the river). The first route was more or less the same as it is today, except for a few renovated houses and the Babuino fountain in a niche of the Palazzo Buoncompagni-Cerasi on the left.

The long and narrow Corso, on the other hand, has undergone a lot of changes since those times. It used to be completely closed in by old houses and was criss-crossed by narrow alleys (to the right Via della Frezza, Via dei Quattro Cantoni and Via del Macello instead of Via Tomacelli). A grand hotel, the Albergo di Roma, was in the Palazzo Lozzano – now the Plaza.

Piazza S. Carlo was then a real piazza whereas now, after the demolition of the area around the Mausoleum of Augustus, it is just a part of the Corso.

The Largo Goldoni existed only on the Via Condotti side. In front, instead of the Palazzo Boncompagni, stood a neo-classical building aligned with the Palazzo Ruspoli. The 'Scalinone' – a large step high enough for watching the carnival processions – has since disappeared underneath the Palazzo Ruspoli (though a few traces remain). On the corner here was the famous Café Nuovo.

The nineteenth century facade of the Palazzo Fiano-Almagià did not yet exist in its present form – and several rather untidy and uninteresting buildings stood in its place.

The major innovations are to be found in the stretch after Via delle Convertite, which has been widened as far as Piazza Sciarra to the width of the square.

The Palazzo Marignoli had not yet been built, nor, of course, had the Rinascente building. Piazza Colonna was closed off on the Galleria side by the Palazzo Boncompagni (Piombino), and the eighteenth century Palazzo Lanci Bonaccorsi by Clemente Orlandi stood in the place of the Banca Commerciale. Via delle Muratte joined the Corso through the Carbognano Arch and Via Marco Minghetti did not exist, since to the side of the Palazzo Sciarra stood the Palazzetto Sciarra, rebuilt in the 1800s. Across the street, the head offices of the Cassa di Risparmio were already being constructed by Antonio Cipolla (1869-74).

On the last stretch of the Corso, which has retained its original layout, the most interesting addition has been the rather obtrusive bulk of the Palazzo Odescalchi by Raffaele Ojetti, but that was only constructed after the fire of 1887; until then only a few modest buildings existed on the site.

Along the Strada Pia

The outer face of Porta Pia had been redesigned, as noted above, by Vespignani under Pius IX. The gate was badly damaged during the assault of the Italian troops in 1870; among other things, the heads were knocked off statues of S. Alessandro and S. Agnese. The troops' first entry-point into the city was not, however, at Porta Pia, but through a gap made in the walls at Villa Paolina, then the property of Prince Napoleon Charles Bonaparte (who was at that time being held captive by the Prussians with his cousin, Napoleon III).

The Via Pia stretched out like a long twisted ribbon, with rustic walls on either side and villas behind. On the right, immediately after the gate, was the Villa Bonaparte; on the left were the Villa Bracciano, and then the British Embassy – that is, the first Villa Torlonia – whose *palazzina* by Antonio Sarti faced onto the road. Still closed in on both sides by the walls of the villas, the road continued down to the beautiful travertine and brick facade of the Granary of Urban VIII. Built by Marcantonio Andreucci in 1640, this was demolished a few decades ago and replaced by the Palazzo di Vetro (or the 'Glass Palace'). Then came the churches: S. Maria della Vittoria, S. Susanna and, near the Acqua Felice fountain, S. Bernardo.

On the right was the Vicolo Sterrato (Vicolo di S. Nicola da Tolentino) which, after 1864, had become an important route connecting the centre with the new Termini Station. (Near to S. Nicola da Tolentino the grand Albergo Costanzi was built – now the Collegio Germanico). On the left, where the Ministry of Defence is today, were no less than three churches all now demolished – S. Caio, SS. Incarnazione (with the monastery of the Barberini), and S. Teresa delle Carmelitane Scalze. And in front was the Barberini garden with the 'sferisterio' – used for the traditional Tuscan game of ball and armlet.

After the Quattro Fontane on the right, came the Papal Palace, and on the left a row of churches, convents and monasteries: S. Carlino dei Trinitari Spagnoli, SS. Anna e Giovacchino dei Carmelitani Scalzi and S. Andrea with its Jesuit Seminary. Two other churches – S. Chiara with its Capuchin monastery and S. Maria Maddalena delle Sacramentate – stood on the site of the public gardens.

The Piazza del Quirinale had recently been levelled in an important project by Vespignani and inaugurated by the Pope himself. ('How much would it cost to change it all back to how it was?', Pius IX is supposed to have asked, jokingly, afterwards). The Pope had also improved access to the Quirinale from the Via Dataria (which used to climb right up to the piazza where the steps now are), where the Palazzo S. Felice (1863-64) and the Palazzo della Dataria (1860-61) had been built. Access to the Quirinale from what is now Via XXIV Maggio was practically non-existent, given the narrowness of the street, and the level of the ground was so much higher then that the Colonna garden did not need steps. At the end of the piazza was the facade of S. Silvestro al Quirinale, now completely altered and relegated to the first floor of an apparently modern building.

Before the construction of the Via del Tritone

Until the end of the 1800s there was no direct road between Piazza Colonna and Piazza Barberini. There was no Largo Chigi and a very small street – the Vicolo Cacciabove – led from the facade of the Palazzo Chigi towards Piazza Colonna, but stopped in the middle of the facade of S. Maria in Via. To the left of the church was the narrow Vicolo del Mortaro, which continued to Piazza Poli. From here one could turn towards either the Via del Pozzetto or the Piazza dei Cruciferi, but the route towards the Tritone was blocked by the Palazzo Poli (by Martino Longhi the Elder, and today largely demolished), and by the Palazzo Comaro (by Giacomo Del Duca, and also much altered and damaged).

The one main arterial road of that area – from the Trevi fountain to the Piazza Barberini – was joined at the crossroads with Via del Nazareno. It consisted of Via della Stamperia, Via dell'Angelo Custode and Via della Madonna di Constantinopoli – the latter two would take the name of the Via del Tritone. Going up this road from the Trevi fountain, one passed on the right what is now the palazzo of the Accademia di S. Luca – formerly the Carpegna – and which in the nineteenth century belonged to the family of Count Luigi Pinciani, the first Mayor of Rome. On the left were the Palazzo della Calcografia by Luigi M. Valadier and the Palazzo Cornaro by Giacomo Del Duca. On reaching the present day Via del Tritone, there were the Collegio Nazareno (by Sebastiano Cipriani, 1698-1712), the Palazzo De Angelis and the Church of S. Maria d'Itria di Constantinopoli. On the right were the Church of the Angelo Custode (by Felice della Greca, with facade by Mattia De Rossi) and the Palazzo Alberoni, both demolished in 1928 to make way for the INA building, set back from the road. Along the last stretch of the Via del Tritone, where it led into Piazza Barberini, and in the piazza itself, there were just a few ordinary buildings. But through the gateway by Pietro da Cortona appeared one of the many contrasts which made the Rome cityscape so fascinating – the main entrance to the 'royal' residence of the Barberini. This most original of Bernini's creations was set off to its best advantage by the low-key, subdued environment around the Fontana del Tritone.

Piazza Barberini was crossed, as it is now, by the Via Felice (ie. Sistina-Quattro Fontane-Depretis). The Fontana delle Api, which acted as a watering trough for horses, stood on the corner of the Via Sistina. Only the first stretch of Via Veneto existed – as an elm grove belonging to the Capuchin church. On the right, where the Fontana delle Api has now been relocated, there was a wooden cross with a base of *cipollino* marble designed by Bertel Thorvaldsen, who had his studios nearby.

At the end of the avenue, on the corner of the Via S. Isidoro, stood the eighteenth century Capuchin bell tower, demolished when the Via Veneto was opened up: the road was then blocked by the Capuchins' kitchen gardens and the Villa Ludovisi. Other roads at the time were the Via S. Basilio and the Via S. Nicola da Tolentina – the first continued into the Via Friuli, where the main entrance of the Villa Ludovisi was located and then went on, more or less following the course of the modern Via Buoncampagni and Via Calabria, up to the Porta Salaria, skirting the Villa Ludovisi on the left. This used to be one of the most beautiful villas in Rome, dating from the 1600s and extended by the addition of other villas (Orsini, Capponi, Altieri, Verospi and Borioni), until it covered an area of almost 247,000 square metres, before falling prey to the property speculators in 1885.

The fore-runners of the Via Nazionale

Since 1864, all Rome's railway stations had been connected at Termini – first in the modest structure built for the Rome-Ceprano railway and then in the building by Salvatore Bianchi, which lasted up until the construction of the present-day station. The building of the station, which at the time appeared quite courageous and in which many private interests were involved, led to the development of a large area previously occupied by villas and vineyards and the creation of a new main road into the centre. This was the Via Nuova Pia – later renamed the Via Nazionale. Meanwhile, in the Castro Pretorio area, where the Jesuit Seminary's vineyards were, Mons. De Meroda was building a large military barracks. Thus began the ruin of the Villa Peretti-Montalto-Massimo, which used to stretch from Via Marsala to Via Depretis and from Via Nazionale to Porta S. Lorenzo. In 1870 the Palazzo Felice and the Palazzo a Termini were still standing (the latter on the site of the Istituto Massimo); both were destroyed between 1886 and 1887.

The mostra of the Acqua Pia (Marcia) originally stood in the vicinity of the Esedra di Termini, where it had been installed by Pius IX on the eve of the occupation of Rome. It was later placed on axis with the Via Nazionale.

But the most important achievement of the time around 1870 was the opening up of the Via Nuova Pia. Private interests were also involved here, but that the work was undertaken with a breadth of vision unusual in those times was largely thanks to the efforts of Mons. Francesco Saverio De Merode, acting Minister to Pius IX's army. He had bought the lands around the Esedra and the Villa Strozzi (linked with the memory of Vittorio Alfieri's sojourn in Rome), and which extended from the Esedra to the Via Viminale and the Via Depretis, and planned their development with a street 22 metres wide on axis with the Esedra and leading to Via Boschetto and with other minor cross streets, one of which would go from Piazza Esquilino to the church of S. Susanna, as the Via Torino does now.

To encourage development of the area, De Merode offered the lots at just 50 centesimi a square metre, but in spite of such favourable conditions, by 1870 only three buildings had been erected on the Via Nazionale in 1870. One of these – number 5, on the corner of Via Torino – still bears a plaque inscribed: 'The first building erected in this quarter between 1868-70'.

The Via Nazionale was to meet up with the already-existing Via di S. Vitale which, following a slightly different route from now, used to link Via Quattro Fontane with the crossraads at Via della Consultavia dei Serpenti. The intended route was already suggested by a small alley (Via Mazzarino), which marked the boundary of the Villa Rospigliosi and then turned towards S. Agata dei Goti. This last section is still here today and retains the name of the famous French-Italian cardinal.

On to the Villa Aldobrandini, whose frontage on the Via Nazionale has since been moved back. The Largo Magnanopoli was an important junction even then; there one joined the only important road in the area – the Via Panisperna – which linked the old centre with S. Maria Maggiore.

A rather narrow road noted earlier used to climb up towards the Quirinal along the route of the Via XXIV Maggio, while Via Panisperna went straight down to Trajan's Forum, following what is now Via Magnanopoli with its steps. Via IV Novembre was still unheard of in 1870 – instead there were the very narrow street called the Via dei Colonnesi and the Via della Pilotta, which made up much of the route. But the Via delle Tre Cannelle did exist, taking a very tortuous route down to the Piazza di SS. Apostoli.

The Capitoline Hill and surrounding area

In 1870 the Capitoline Hill still marked the boundary between town and countryside. A tree-lined avenue crossed the Campo Vaccino (the area of the ancient forum), where a few excavations had already been carried out. The most renowned ruins in the world were set in a rural scene, the most lively components of which were long lines of washing drying in the sun, rope-makers at work, stationary farm carts and drowsy oxen.

A monumental gateway in a fortified wall served as an entrance to the Palatine and to the Farnese gardens, which then belonged to Napoleon III. Beyond the Arch of Titus and the Colosseum, a broad road, the Stradone di S. Giovanni, led to the Lateran, but the Caelian Hill was just a sea of green through which churches and scattered ruins could be seen, and beyond the walls, the real countryside.

Around the Capitoline, however, was a densely-populated neighbourhood, with many houses clinging to the slopes. At the foot of the steps, the irregularly-shaped Piazza Araecoli was still a good place from which to admire the Capitoline buildings, as Michelangelo had envisaged. The Piazza was surrounded by stately *palazzi* and overlooked by the church of S. Venanzio dei Camerinesi. A road skirted the contours of the hill – off the Piazza Aracoeli was the Via Giulio Romano with its church of S. Rita (since dismantled and moved elsewhere) and the picturesque house, traditionally the birthplace of Raphael's most talented student. Further along was the Palazzo of the Pedacchia family, later bought and restored by Pietro da Cortona. A junction linked this road with Via della Ripresa dei Barberi and Via di Marforio, which led from Piazza Venezia to the Arch of Septimius Severus between the churches of SS. Luca e Martina and of S. Giuseppe dei Falegnami. Here stood the Palazzo Mantica, which housed the remains of the Tomb of Bibulus. Next, one came to the small piazzetta of Macel de' Corvi and the house where Michelangelo died, and finally arrived at Trajan's Forum, where part of the Basilica Ulpia had been excavated during the French administration.

On the opposite side of the Piazza Aracoeli was the Via Tor de' Specchi, with the little churches of S. Andrea in Vincis and of SS. Orsola e Caterina. This led on to the Piazza Montanara, dominated by the bulky Palazzo Orsini. The fountain in the middle of the piazza was where farm labourers used to come to look for employment. The piazza was surrounded by modest inns and every sort of workshop and trade. Further down, in a quiet little square, was the church of S. Nicola in Carcere.

Continuing on a tour around the Capitoline, one would come to the Via della Consolazione which, passing the church of S. Omobono on the right, led to the Piazza della Consolazione. From here, by going along the Corsia dell'Ospedale, one arrived at the Campo Vaccino.

From Piazza Montanara a road went up to the top of the Capitoline passing beneath the Arch of the Saponari and in front of the Church of S. Maria in Vincis. The huge German Archaeological Institute had not yet been built, but there were other German buildings in the area, such as the Villa Caffarelli, the Ospedale Teutonica and the Casa Tarpea – the old seat of the Istituto di Correspondenza Archeologica.

On the other side of the hill, where the Victor Emmanuele monument now stands, was the massive tower of Paul III. Connected to Piazza Venezia by a viaduct, this used to be the summer residence of the Pope, and was later the seat of the Curia Generalizia dei Frati Minori (General Council of Lay-Brothers). All round were the now-demolished buildings and secluded cloisters of the Aracoeli monastery, and the famous botanical library. There were two means of access to the Capitoline by carriage – the Via delle Tre Pile, dating from the end of the 1600s, led up from Piazza Aracoeli, while the other, built during the French administration, went from the Campo Vaccino and passed over the Portico degli Dei Consenti. This remained in use until the excavations at the end of the nineteenth century.

From Piazza Venezia to St Peter's

The Piazza Venezia was half the size it is today. One can get a good idea of its dimensions before 1900 by standing in the middle of the square and extending imaginary lines from the houses on the right of the Corso and from the church of S. Marco, to the side of the Palazzo Venezia. The square was dominated by this Palazzo, and closed off on the side where the monument now stands by the *palazzetto*, and on the left by the Palazzo Bolognetti, which had been given a splendid nineteenth century interior by the Torlonia family. The Corso used to extend down towards Macel de' Corvi by means of Via della Ripresa dei Barbari, where a big awning strung out across the street would mark the finishing post of the famous horse-race without jockeys. It was this race, from Piazza del Popolo to Piazza Venezia, which gave the Corso its name. The races continued until 1885.

The quickest route to St. Peter's began in Via del Gesù (now the Via del Plebiscito) – a long narrow piazza rather than a road which, then as now, skirted Piazza Venezia. Beyond the narrow alley between Via del Gesù and the Palazzo Altieri, the road met the ancient Via Papale, which led to the Capitoline. The first stretch of the Corso Vittorio Emanuele used to be very narrow and was later widened on the right by 16 metres. This involved the sacrifice of a few buildings, including the Palazzo Amadei, where Giuseppe Giachino Belli died. The road continued straight down along what is now the Largo di Torre Argentina, leading into the Via del Sudario and turning first to one side and then in front of the church of S. Andrea della Valle, where the Piazza della Valle is today.

Going back to what is now the Largo di Torre Argentina, it is worth remembering that the Via Arenula is a recent creation of post 1886. Instead, the Via di Torre Argentina used to go past the Argentina Theatre and the Palazzo Cesarini and arrive in Piazza S. Elena opposite the church of S. Elena dei Credenzieri. It was joined on the left by the Via delle Botteghe Oscure-Florida. Travelling on towards the Tiber one passed the now-demolished church of S. Anna dei Falegnami and its Benedictine monastery, and past the junction with the Via dei Falegnami to arrive at Piazza di Branca (later enlarged and renamed after Benedetto Cairoli). From here the new street was widened to lead down among the old houses to the river.

Returning to the Piazza della Valle, this is where the narrow Via di S. Pantaleo began, curving out in front of the Palazzo Massimo to arrive at the Piazza di S. Pantaleo, and continuing along its current route up to Piazza Pasquino. From here, the Via Papale linked the Via del Governo Vecchio, Piazza dell'Orologio and the Via Banchi Nuovi. At the end of this street stood the Palazzo della Zecca Vecchia by Antonio da Sangallo the Younger (trapezoidal in shape) where it formed the corner of two streets the Via Papale and the Via Banchi Vecchi. The Via Papale continued on to the Banco di S. Spirito, crossed the river by the Ponte S. Angelo and ran first through the Borgo to arrive, of course, at St. Peter's. Going back to the Piazza S. Pantaleo, let us try to immagine the former state of the Corso Vittorio. No one street existed along this stretch; instead, a series of narrow streets and alleys ran in the same direction as the present-day artery. The Piazza di Sora, on the same alignment, was overlooked by the old Palazzo Fieschi-Buoncompagni, nowadays much changed and the seat of the Gioberti Institute. The modern-day Corso Vittorio destroyed a fine sixteenth century *palazzo* to cut through to the Piazza della Chiesa Nuova, the Piazza Sforza Cesarini and then across the ancient garden of the Palazzo Sforza Cesarini. Still following a new route without ancient precedents, the Corso then intersects with Via del Consolato and Via Paola, to arrive at the Tiber near to where the Ponte Neroniano used to stand.

Although the passage of the new Corso Vittorio through Rioni (districts) V and VI undoubtably severely damaged the appearance of the old city centre, no exeptionally precious buildings were sacrificed, and the operation was completed successfully enough. Among the losses were the Palazzo Bini in Via del Consolato, the church of S. Maria della Purificazione, the church of S. Orsola della Pietà; the Palazzo del Consolato dei Fiorentini and other less important buildings.

The 'crown of villas'

One of the most notable characteristics of Rome was the 'radiant crown of noble villas to which nothing in the world of reminiscence or poetry can compare' (D'Annunzio). This used to girdle the medieval city, both inside and outside the walls. Beginning with the Villa Ludovisi, which extended as far as Piazza Fiume, and continuing to the right, one came to the Villa Mandosi (near Piazza Sallustio), the Villa Barberini (later Spithoever) along the Strada Pia, and then, beyond Via di Porta Salaria, to the triangular site of the Villa Bonaparte between Porta Salaria and Via XX Settembre.

On the other side of the Via XX Settembre were the Villa Costaguti-Bracciano (the British Embassy) the Villas Alberini, Olgiati, Piondini, Lattanzi, De Vecchi and Martini, which led one down to Porta S. Lorenzo and the enormous Villa Montalto (later Negroni and Massimo), which extended down from the Esquiline Hill. Around S. Bibiana were the Villa Sacripante and the Villa Magnani. And on the Esquiline Hill, near S. Maria Maggiore, were the Caetani (Caserta) villa at. S. Vito, the Villa Palombara (later Massimo), at Piazza Vittorio Emmanuele II, and the villa Altieri, a small part of which remains near the Via Labicana.

Next came the Villa Giustiniani (later Massimo), near S. Antonio da Padova, the Villa Astalli and the Villa Wolkonsky (now the residence of the British Ambassador).

Most of the Caelian Hill was taken up by the Villa Fonseca (between Via della Ferratella and Via S. Stefano Rotondo) and the Villa Casali (later the military hospital). There was also the Villa Campana along the Stradone di S. Giovanni, which housed the Marchese Campana's famous collection of antiquities until most of it was bought by Napoleon III. The remainder of the Caelian was occupied by the surviving Villa Mattei. The great loop of the ancient city walls from Porta S. Sebastiano around the Aventine to Testaccio, was for the most part planted with vines – and some still survive in the Villa del Priorato di Malta. Up on the Janiculum were the Villa Ottoboni, the Villa Crescenzi (later Barberini, Sciarra and Wurts), and the Villa Spada, the Farnese-Savorelli (now Aurelia), the Corsini and the Cesi. Finally there were the Vatican Gardens.

Outside the Walls, to mention, only a few, were the Villa Borghese, the Villa Albani, the Villa Chigi (now in a very poor state), the Gangalandi-Lancellotti (a fraction of which has been preserved), the Patrizi (destroyed), Bolognetti (also destroyed), Torlonia, Alberoni (now Paganini) and, on the Janiculum, the Giraud (Vascello), Doria Pamphilj and Ferroni (later Valentini and Abamelek).

A characteristic feature of the villa district were the high, round-topped walls, interrupted every so often by imposing gates. The Via di Porta S. Sebastiano and the Via Porta Latina give an impression of what the roads of the Esquiline Hill or the Viminale looked like up until 1870.

The most important villas were open to the public on certain days (e.g. the Villa Borghese), or by special permit (e.g. the Villa Ludovisi). The only public park was that on the Pincian Hill but the meadows of the Popolo Romano in Testaccio, with their open-air taverns, provided a popular venue for the 'Ottobrate' or October fairs.

The nearby 'English' cemetery by the Pyramid of Cestius contrasted with such revelry, but at the same time was so picturesque that Shelley wrote of it: 'One could fall in love with death at the thought of being buried in such an enchanting place'.

The Jewish quarter

Since 1848 the *Ghetto* and ceased to be a ghetto in literal terms. However, many Jews continued to live in the area in which they had been confined for three centuries – in spite of the fact that it had got steadily smaller and smaller, even with Leo XII's efforts to enlarge it by the addition of the Via della Reginella and part of the Via della Pescheria. Conditions have changed dramatically since 1888, when the quarter was almost completely demolished and rebuilt, but it is still a traditionally Jewish neighbourhood. Old photographs provide a vivid picture of the incredibly tightly-packed existence of the inhabitants of these three hectares.

The ghetto was crossed by three streets running more or less parallel with the Tiber. The main one was the Via Rua, which started in the Piazza Giudea (Piazza di Mercatello); a second one was composed of a patchwork of little streets and alleyways and began in the Piazza delle Scole behind the Vicolo Cenci, passing the *piazzette* dei Macelli and delle Tre Cannelle to finish up in the Via delle Azimelli, Vicolo della Torre, Vicolo dei Savelli and Vicolo dei Quattro Capi. The last of the three roads followed the banks of the river and was therefore subject to flooding – this was the Via della Fiumara, whose houses reached right down to the river's edge.

In the Piazza delle Scole there were the five Scholae – or schools – the Temple, the Catalan, the Sicilian, the Castillian and the New. These were all demolished in 1910, though much of the furniture and fittings survives.

Just outside the Jewish Quarter were some of the most picturesque parts of the old city: the Pescheria (the old fish market), which since medieval times had nestled between the arches and columns of the Portico d'Ottavia; the Piazza Giudea, with its sixteenth century fountain; Monte Cenci, and the Theatre of Marcellus, whose buried arcades had been turned into shops.

Life was incredibly active in this cramped area, in spite of the severe poverty, which created striking contrasts with the grand ruins of the past.

Trastevere

It is difficult for us to imagine Trastevere without the Ponte Garibaldi and the Viale di Trastevere, which were both constructed after 1870. There used to be four routes into the district – the Porta Settimiana, the Ponte Sisto, the Tiber Island bridges and the Ponte Rotto, which Pius IX had joined once more the ancient Forum Boarium.

The Ponte Rotto led on one side to the Piazza S. Maria in Trastevere and on the other to S. Cecilia and the Hospice of S. Michele. The Ponte Sisto, too, led to Piazza S. Maria in Trastevere, and from there the Stradone di S. Francesco a Ripa led on to the Ripagrande area and marked the boundary of the old city. The monastery of S. Cosimato stood in open farmland which stretched right up to S. Maria in Trastevere and S. Egidio. Access to the Janiculum was from the Via delle Fornaci (now Via Garibaldi) by means of the new road built by Pius IX.

The change which had the greatest impact on the area during Pius' pontificate was the construction of the Tobacco Factory, with the creation of the Piazza Mastai in front and the new access road from the Via S. Francesco a Ripa, with Busiri's enormus *propylaea*.

The present-day Viale di Trastevere has sliced right across this new artery with its double line of trees, radically altering Busiri's scheme.

In these pages we have tried to paint a picture of the city as it must have appeared to the Italian troops entering Rome on 20 September 1870. Just a little remains to be said about the actors who animated the scene.

Silvio Negro, in his *Seconda Roma*, has written very vividly of the city in the last decades of Papal Rome, and few others have come close to the flavour and character captured in this summary: 'The first and strongest impressions aroused by the Rome of that time were born out of anachronisms and the play of contrasts. It was still a city in costume – not in the simple sense of its outward appearance, but rather in the manner in which the way of life was still determined by fixed rules and customs, preserved in equal measure by the theological government and the naturally conservative Roman temperament.

'The imagination was stirred by the contrasts between the ruins of pagan Rome and the Baroque invasion of the later Christian city; between monuments renowned throughout the world and the shoe-makers and food stalls lodged between their arcades; between the top-hatted Englishman out sightseeing, followed two paces behind by his servant carrying the guidebook, and the goatherd asleep on the pavement near his herd; between the majestic and at times overpowering weight of history and the vigorous and unpretentious mentality which could make a barn out of an ancient tomb or turn a sarcophagus into a watering hole; between the pomp and ceremony of the Catholic metropolis which was still the grail of many pilgrims and visitors, and the rough market town of a countryside inhabited by some of the most violent people in Italy, and where one could easily die of malaria...'

Of this dramatic scenario, made even more exciting by the contrasts highlighted by Silvio Negro, Robert Macpherson's photographs form one of the earliest, richest and most treasured records.

Carlo Pietrangeli

BIBLIOGRAPHY

General sources of information:
Istituto di Studi Romani, *Mostra di Roma nell'Ottocento,* Rome, 1932.
C. Pietrangeli, *Il Museo di Roma: documenti e iconografia* (Roma Cristiana, XV), Bologna, 1971.

Newspapers:
Album (l'), 1834-1862. Rome.
Buonarroti (Il), 1866 segg. Rome.
Giornale Arcadico di scienze, lettere ed arti, 1819-1868. Rome.
Diario ordinario, 1716-1848. Rome.
Gazzetta di Roma, 1848-1849. Rome.
Monitore Romano, 1849. Rome.
Giornale di Roma, 1849-1870. Rome.
Notizie per l'anno... 1716-1860 e *Annuario Pontificio* 1860-1870.

History:
L.F.N. Besson, *Frédéric François-Xavier de Merode, Ministre de Pie IX...* Paris, 1886.
D. Silvagni, *La corte e la società romana nei secoli XVIII e XIX,* Roma 1883-85 (reprinted by L. Felici, Rome 1971).
R. De Cesare, *Roma e lo Stato del Papa dal ritorno di Pio IX al XX settembre,* Rome 1907.
Alfonso Ventrone, *L'Amministrazione dello Stato Pontificio dal 1848 al 1870,* Rome, 1942.
S. Negro, *Seconda Roma (1850-1870),* first edition, Milan 1943.
P. Dalla Torre, *L'opera riformatrice ed amministrativa di Pio IX tra il 1850 e il 1870,* Rome (1945).
F. Hayward, *Pie IX et son temps,* Paris, 1948.
R. Aubert, *Le pontificat de Pie IX,* Paris, 1952.
G. Martina, *Pio IX,* Rome, 1974-85.
F. Bartoccini, *Roma nell'Ottocento,* Bologna, 1985 (*Storia di Roma* Istituto di Studi Romani, XVI).

Memoirs and Diaries:
E. About, *Rome contemporaine,* Paris, 1860.
L. Veuillot, *Le parfum de Rome,* Paris, 1862.
W.B. Story, *Roba de Roma,* London, 1864.
H. Taine, *Voyage en Italie: Naples et Rome,* Paris, 1866.
L. Delatre, *Ricordi di Roma,* Florence, 1870.
A. Herzen, *Lettres de France et d'Italie* (1842-1852), Geneva, 1871.
A. Bresciani, *Edmondo o dei Costumi del Popolo Romano,* Milan, 1872.
H. d'Ideville, *Journal d'un diplomate en Italie. Notes intimes pour servir à l'histoire du Second Empire à Rome,* 1862-66, Paris, 1873.
F. Wey, *Rome. Descriptions et souvenirs,* Paris, 1873.
Diario di Nicola Roncalli dall'anno 1849 al 1870 introduced by a historical study by R. Ambrosi de Magistris and I. Ghironi about Italian Unity, Turin 1884. (The still unpublished diary is preserved in the Istituto Italiano per la Storia del Risorgimento in Rome).
F. Gregorovius, *Römische Tagebücher,* Stuttgart, 1892.
Diario del principe Don Agostino Chigi, dal 1830 al 1855, introduced by an essay on historic curiosities collected by Cesare Fraschetti concerning life in Rome in the first decades of the 19th century. (The handwritten diary comprises 21 volumes).
Nassau G. Senior, *Italy after 1848,* Bari, 1937.

Topography, town-planning and architecture:
P. Cacchiatelli - G. Cleter, *Le scienze e le arti sotto il pontificato di Pio IX,* second edition, 1865.
Triplice omaggio alla Santità di Papa Pio IX nel suo Giubileo Episcopale offerto dalle tre romane accademie..., Rome, 1877.
G.B. Florio, *Raccolta completa di Regolamenti edilizi e norme riguardanti la città di Roma dal 1864 ad oggi.* Rome, 1931.
Regolamento edilizio e di pubblico ornato per la città di Roma, April 1864.
Regolamento sulle altezze delle fabbriche e sull'ampiezza de' cortili nell'interno della città di Roma, 21 November 1866.

G. Giovannoni, in F. Castagnoli, C. Cecchelli, G. Giovannoni, M. Zocca, *Topografia e urbanistica di Roma,* Rocca S. Casciano, 1958 (*Storia di Roma* Istituto di Studi Romani, XXII).
G. Spagnesi, *La Roma di Pio IX: l'immagine della città,* in *Cento anni di architettura a Roma 1870-1970,* catalogue, Rome, 1971.
G. Spagnesi, *Edilizia romana nella seconda metà del secolo XIX (1848-1905),* Rome, 1974.
G. Spagnesi, *L'architettura a Roma al tempo di Pio IX (1830-1870),* Rome, 1976.
L. Gallo, *Indice analitico del Fondo "Titolo 54" (1848-1870). Sussidi per la consultazione dei fondi urbanistici ed edilizi dell'Archivio Capitolino,* in *Architettura e Archivi - fonti e storia,* 1982, pp. 57-84.

Guides to Rome:
A. Nibby, *Itinerario di Roma e delle sue vicinanze,* Rome, 1824.
C. Fea, *Descrizione di Roma antica e moderna,* Rome 1834. (expanded edition by Mercuri in 1856).
Corografia di Roma ovvero descrizione e cenni storici dei suoi monumenti colla guida dei medesimi mercé di linee stradali, ecc., Rome, 1846.
A. Rufini, *Dizionario etimologico-storico delle strade, piazze caffè, alberghi e locande esistenti nella città di Roma,* Rome, 1847.
A. Rufini, *Notizie storiche intorno all'origine di alcune osterie, caffè, alberghi e locande esistenti nella città di Roma,* Rome, 1855.
A. Rufini, *Guida di Roma e dei suoi dintorni,* Rome, 1857.
G. Melchiorri, *Guida metodica di Roma e suoi contorni,* Rome 1868.

Maps and views (drawings, engravings, lithographs):
Rome dans sa grandeur d'après nature per Philippe Benoist *et* Felix Benoist ecc., 3 vols., Paris, 1870.
P. Arrigoni e A. Bertarelli, *Piante e vedute di Roma e del Lazio conservate nella raccolta delle stampe e dei disegni del Castello Sforzesco,* Milan, 1939.
Istituto di Studi Romani, *Le piante di Roma,* ed. by A.P. Frutaz, III vol., Roma, 1962.

Medals:
A. Patrignani, *Le medaglie di Pio IX,* (Extract from the journal of the Circolo Numismatico Napoletano)
A. Rinaldi, *Catalogo delle medaglie papali da Pio VII a Paolo VI,* Verona, 1967.
F. Bortolotti, *Le medaglie annuali dei romani pontefici (1605-1967),* Rimini, 1967.
F. Bortolotti, *Le medaglie pontificie di massimo modulo da Pio IX a Pio XI,* Rimini, 1971.
T. Turco, *Medaglie di massimo modulo coniate a Roma nel pontificato di Pio IX,* Rome, 1977.
Comitato Celebrazioni Centenarie (1878-1978), *Pio IX nelle monete e nelle medaglie,* Rome, 1979.
Istituto Poligrafico dello Stato: *L'arte della medaglia e della moneta nelle opere della Zecca di Stato dal 1846,* Rome, 1980.

Photographs of Rome:
Mostra della fotografia a Roma dal 1840 al 1915, catalogue, Rome, 1953.
S. Negro, *Album romano,* Florence, 1956.
S. Negro, *Nuovo Album romano,* ed. by L. Negro e C. Pietrangeli, Piacenza, 1964.
Roma cento anni fa nelle fotografie del tempo, catalogue, Rome, 1971.
Le fotografie di Enrico Valenziani, Catalogue ed. by P. Becchetti, Florence, 1975.
B. Brizzi, *Roma cento anni fa nelle fotografie della raccolta Parker,* Rome, 1975.
V. Cianfarani, *Immagini romane,* Rome, 1976.
Roma dei fotografi al tempo di Pio IX 1846-1878, catalogue, Rome, 1977.
Rome in early Photographs: 1846-1878, the age of Pius IX, Copenaghen 1977, also published in German *Rom in frühen Photographien 1846-1878,* Munich, 1978.
A.N. *Normand architecte, Photographies 1851-52,* Rome, 1978.
L. Vitali, *Il Risorgimento nella fotografia,* Turin, 1979.
P. Becchetti - C. Pietrangeli, *Roma in dagherrotipia,* Rome, 1979.
P. Becchetti, *La fotografia a Roma dalle origini al 1915,* Rome, 1983.
Pittori fotografi a Roma 1845-1870, catalogue, Rome 1987.

ROBERT MACPHERSON THE PHOTOGRAPHER

The history of photography is dotted with the names of those who, either by their inventions or revolutionary new methods, have contributed towards the technical and aesthetic perfection of this relatively recent art form. To this famous list must now be added the long-neglected name of Robert Macpherson. This fascinating and impressive character worked as a photographer in Rome for over 20 years during the last century, and left behind him a body of work which, though small, makes up for in aesthetic and poetic quality what it lacks in quantity.

Robert Macpherson was born in Edinburgh in 1815[1], a direct descendent of James Macpherson, the well-known translator of Ossian. He studied medicine for several years with the intention of setting himself up as a surgeon in India. But when he left Britain in 1840, reasons which included his health and artistic inclinations led him instead to Rome, where he took up the more appealing profession of painter[2].

To appreciate Macpherson's work and his pioneering role in the history of photography, it is necessary to take a close look at his life, particularly the 33 years spent in Rome[3].

There is certainly no lack of sources here – he is mentioned in many books, periodicals, newspapers, biographies and letters, all of which combine to build up a picture of his life. It is also necessary to say something about the world in which he lived – that of the artists, photographers, intellectuals, aristocrats, foreigners and antiquarians who had made their home in Rome. For the city was not only the world capital of Christianity; it was also, of course, an important cultural centre.

The most valuable of all the memoirs of the time are those of the American painter, James Edward Freeman (1808-84), who had lived in Rome for a long time and was a close friend of Macpherson's[4]. They met for the first time in the Doria Pamphilj Gallery, where Macpherson was copying a picture by Lorenese, and the friendship was cemented when, on returning to Rome in 1841, Freeman found Macpherson among the painting students who had enrolled in his absence.

1. Until now his date of birth was assumed to be in 1811, but various Roman archives, including the *Stati delle Anime* (or parish records) and his death certificate, suggest that he was born in either 1815 or 1815. See also no. 16.

2. See the obituary in the *British Journal of Photography*, 6 December 1872.

3. His long residence in Rome is recorded in many documents: in 1841 he lived at no, 38, Via Gregoriana (see H. Le Grice, Walks *through the Studios of the Sculptors in Rome* etc. Puccinelli, Rome, 1841, p. 280); in 1846 at no. 6, Via della Croce (see *The Roman Advertiser*, Rome, 24 October 1846); in 1848 at no. 54, Via Gregoriana (see *The Roman Advertiser*, Rome, 28 Oct 1848 and 30 Dec 1848); in 1854 at no. 44, Via dei Greci (see the *Stato delle Anime* of the parish of S. Giacomo in Augusta, 1854; in 1856 he had a studio at no. 4 Via degli Strozzi (see *Murray's Handbook* of 1856); in 1856 at no. 192, Via di Ripetta (see printed catalogue of Macpherson's photographs, 1858); in 1863 he moved his studio to no. 12, Vicolo d'Alibert, which later became his home when he transferred his studio to no. 57 Via di Campo Marzio (formerly Stefano Lais), and later to Via Flaminia, outside the Porta del Popolo at the Vigna Poniatowski (see printed catalogue of 1863, the *Stato delle Anime* of the parish of S. Maria del Popolo for the years in question and the *Guida Monaci* for the years 1871-74).

4. See James Edward Freeman, *Gatherings from an Artist's Portfolio*, New York, Appleton and Company, 1877, vol I and *Gatherings from an Arist's Portfolio in Rome*, Boston, 1883.

Freeman's memoirs tell how, on that first meeting, 'Mac', as he was known, was wearing a kilt. This had attracted a lot of attention, he noted, regardless of the fact that to most nineteenth century visitors to Rome, the whole city must have seemed like a fancy dress parade. But Freeman goes on to say how well the outfit suited Macpherson, with his tall, strong build and well-shaped, agile legs, and described him as having a thick head of red hair[5], clear blue eyes, fine features and a rosy, fresh complexion. Besides these physical gifts, the artist was also extremely charming, a sound judge of character, and possessed an incredible memory, great powers of description and, above all, a quick and easy sense of humour.

This combination of qualities meant that Macpherson could always count on the friendship of some of the most prominent names of the British aristocracy, such as the Marquis of Northampton, the Duke of Hamilton and Count Dudley. In addition, his conversion to Catholicism opened up the doors of the most exclusive Roman society, where frequently no amount of noble blood or wealth alone was enough to secure an entry. Macpherson was also a regular *habitué* of the Café Greco, where he would sit like a king on a throne and greet everyone as they came in.

Such a dizzy social whirl would have turned many people's heads, but it had no effect whatsoever on Macpherson's character. Indeed, the only harm done was to his studies – as he devoted more time to his social life than to his painting. Macpherson was both intelligent and artistically gifted, but he lacked powers of concentration. Too frequently, rather than staying at home and grappling with the technicalities of anatomy, perspective or composition, he would allow himself to be tempted away by friends who desired his excellent company at lunch or dinner, or for trips to the country side or to other parts of Italy.

But Macpherson's life underwent a profound change after the arrival in Rome of Anna Jameson (1794-1860) the famous English writer, and her neice and *protegée*, Geraldine Bate[6]. 'Geddie', as her family called her, was an exceptionally charming and lively girl, and on meeting her, Mac fell hopelessly in love. Fortunately, Geddie returned the Scottish artist's affections, and the two were married in England. The wedding presents included a silver dinner service from Lady Byron, the wife of the famous poet, while the Duke of Hamilton had the couple to stay in his magnificent country house.

A letter written by Anna Jameson to Catherine Sedwick on 10 October 1849, reports that: 'My niece Geraldine married Robert Macpherson on 4 September. He is an artist from a good Highland family, and is a good, gentle and honest man. I will admit to having been against the match at first, but what seemed to be just infatuation has become admirable for the constancy of affection on both sides, and I am glad that I gave my consent. They are at present in Scotland, and will return to Rome in about three weeks'[7].

Marriage to the favourite neice of Anna Jameson meant that Macpherson was now also welcomed in the *salons* of literary celebrities living in Rome, such as the Brownings. He also became a close friend of W. M. Thackeray[8], who lived in the Via Condotti, right opposite the Café Greco, when in Rome. Macpherson was also to become a regular visitor at the home of the American sculptor, William Wetmore Story, near the Palazzo Barberini. As Diego Angeli

5. At a later date he grew a beard of the same beautiful red colour as his hair.
6. The document in the Rome Registry Office refers rather strangely to: 'Geraldine Beatek, widow of Macpherson', rather than Geraldine Bate.
7. See G. Macpherson, *Memoirs of Anna Jameson*, London, 1878, p. 261.
8. See Obituary, *op. cit.*

remembers, this *salon* was one of the most brilliant Anglo-Italian literary circles that Rome could boast at the time; there was hardly a European or American writer who failed to stop by while passing through Rome. Lord Houghton, the Brownings, Longfellow, Lord Tennyson, Sala and Mrs Gaskell were but a few of those who attended.

After their honeymoon the Macphersons returned to Rome which, contrary to all their original plans, was to become their permanent residence. They were given a warm and affectionate welcome by all their friends[9].

But the first problems were not slow to arrive. Their main obstacle was Macpherson's lack of maturity as a painter, which prevented him from making a viable career from his art. In fact, as Freeman records, the couple were bracing themselves for a very frugal Christmas one year, due to a total lack of funds, only to be saved at the last moment by an English gentleman buying one of Macpherson's antique paintings.

This story brings up the fact that Macpherson was quite a connoisseur of old paintings. This not only meant that he could make ends meet by buying and selling famous works of art; it also led to his discovery of a number of authentic masterpieces, which were later to become noted additions to various collections in Britain.

In Florence once, realising the value of a picture he had seen, Macpherson became the owner of an authentic portrait of Vittorio Colonna by Sebastiano del Piombo, which he then sold, at great profit, to Count Dudley. But his real coup came about during the dispersal of Cardinal Joseph Fesch's renowned collection of over 3,332 pictures. After the cardinal's death in Rome on 13 May 1839, a number of seemingly unremarkable pictures ended up in the cellar of the Palazzo Falconiere. Much later, these were sold by the cardinal's heir, the Prince of Musignano, to a Roman antique dealer called Vito Enei. In 1846 some of the pictures were bought by Macpherson, who was particularly attracted by a large panel covered in dust, through which he could just make out a few figures that seemed to be exceptionally well-painted[10]. As soon as he began to remove the grime accumulated through centuries of neglect, he discovered a magnificent head and figure. Peter Cornelius, who was summoned immediately, attributed them to Michelangelo; this opinion was later confirmed by Federico Overbeck and Tommaso Minardi.

The news of this find flew around Rome in no time and caused quite a furore. As soon as the previous owner came to hear about it, he tried to take Macpherson to court to get the painting back, in spite of the fact that he had already received payment for it. The case carried on for years, with expenses incurred on both sides but was finally settled in favour of Macpherson, who was confirmed as the legal owner. This *Deposition of Christ*, attributed to Michelangelo, was bought in 1868 for the National Gallery in London[11] by Sir William Boxall, who paid just £ 2000 – much less than the picture was worth.

9. From the marriage to Geraldine Bate, Macpherson had five children, all born in Rome. The first, probably born in 1850, died suddenly in Dec. 1852, as is reported in a letter from W. Story to James Russell Lowell on 11 February 1853 (see G. R. Hudson, *Browning to his American Friends: Letters 1841-1890* 1965. p. 271); the second, Guglielmo, was born in 1853, Giuseppe in 1855; Aida in 1861 and Francesco in 1866.

10. Another version of this famous story is told by Cecil Gould. While out taking a walk, Macpherson's attention was caught by the counter of a stallholder who sold old iron, and occasionally food, such as fish. Underneath all the grime and dirt, it seemed to be decorated with painted figures. He managed to buy the counter which, after cleaning off all the dirt, turned out to be a painting by Michelangelo.

11. This painting, as Macpherson often used to say, was 'Geraldine's joy', but economic hardship forced them to sell it.

Macpherson also bought pictures for the National Gallery of Ireland which was founded in Dublin in 1854. The minutes of meetings of the gallery directors are filled with references to a number of paintings bought by, or through, Macpherson in Rome, which were considered the most worthy pictures with which to start up the public collection. During a meeting on 3 November 1856 the decision was made to buy the picture collection of Aducci, a well-known Roman dealer, using Macpherson as the gallery's agent in Rome. To this collection Macpherson added some pictures of his own, including the *Expulsion of Adam and Eve from Paradise* by Mattia Preti, a portrait of Count Alberti by Andrea Celesti and a stunning panorama by Giovanni Battista Viola. Shortly afterwards another remarkable group of paintings was acquired through Macpherson; this included Andrea del Sarto's *Adoration of the Magi*, Andrea Bassano's *Holy Family*, a copy of Correggio's *St Jerome* by Annibale Carracci and *the Martyrdom of St. Sebastian* by Domenichino. Proof of Macpherson's obvious skill is the large number of pictures he bought for the National Gallery of Ireland which are still held in high regard[12].

* * *

According to his friends, there was no house in Rome that was as hospitable as Macpherson's, or at which one could hope to meet such famous and interesting people. There was a constant

12. For more information, see Michael Wynne, *Fesch Paintings in the National Gallery of Ireland* in the *Gazette des Beaux Arts*, January 1977.

coming and going of artists, patrons, visitors from Scotland, Italian and ecclesiastical dignitaries and more or less the entire English-speaking community in Rome.

The cultivated mixture of Scots and Italian in Macpherson's personality and habits made him a particularly charismatic figure[13]. As a family man, he remained very closely attached to the customs of his native land, and as a Catholic, he took an active part in the services and festivals that took place throughout the Christian year. Here, the memories of another of his contemporaries, Charles Mackenzie, are useful. He had arrived in Rome in 1869 and writes of a visit on 17 March of that year to the Church of S. Isidoro degli Irlandesi (in the Via degli Artisti), to celebrate St. Patrick's Day. He remembers Macpherson at the door, handing out shamrocks which had been blessed by the Pope from a large silver dish.[14]

Macpherson had settled in very well in his newly-adopted country. The adaptability and depth of human feeling which helped him to do so are further illustrated by a brief incident that happened near Nemi. The Macphersons had invited the English writer, Mrs. Oliphaunt, to stay with them in Frascati while she got over the death of her daughter. They often went out for long walks together in the beautiful countryside around the town. 'Once', she wrote, 'Robert took me out into the woods near Nemi, where we met a rather rude and untrustworthy-looking group of charcoal burners. It was all rather frightening but, because Robert spoke their dialect and could understand the way they behaved, they soon became quite friendly...'[15]

Robert Macpherson was still very active and full of plans for the future when he was struck down in his studio (at that time just outside the Porta del Popolo in the building next to the Casina Vagnuzzi), by a terrible attack of malaria. He died on 17 November 1872. His death certificate, drawn up by the priest of his local church, S. Maria del Popolo, reads: '*Anno Domini 1872, Die 17.9. bris. In Vinea Puniavtoski extra Portam Flaminiam hora 7 p.m. Sacram. munitus. obiit. III. mus DD Robertus q. Ioannis Macpherson a Scotia Vir Geraldine Bate. Post solemnes exequias cum expositione sepultus est in Pub. o Coemet. in Loculo speciali. Aetatis suae anno 57. In fidem*'[16].

The death of someone as well-known and well-loved as Robert Macpherson was the cause of much grief and distress, particularly in the English-speaking and artistic communities in Rome.

13. See Harry Coghill, *Autobiography and Letters of Mrs M. O. Oliphaunt*, 1899, p. 57.

14. See Charles MacKenzie, *A Trip to Rome*, 1869, pp. 59-60. This 62 page volume was printed privately by R. Clarke, as stated on the title page.

15. See Harry Coghill, *op. cit.* p. 96.

16. See *Liber XIX Mortuorum S. Maria de Populo Urbis ab Anno* 1855, p. 144. The cause of death is given in the general records of the deceased in Rome for the year 1872 as 'perniciosa'. It is recorded that on 21 Nov. 1874, in the same building, the famous Spanish painter, Mariano Fortuni, also died of 'perniciosa'. Following lengthy research at the Verano Cemetery, we were able to locate the place where Macpherson was buried on 19 Nov. 1872 – in niche no. 161, third row. The burial of his wife Geraldine is recorded more clearly, in the death registers of 1878: 'Geraldine Macpherson, buried on 27 May, 1878 in niche no. 161, third row of the Vicolo della Ranocchia, next to her husband'. The Via della Ranocchia was the name given to a group of niches constructed in a bank of three rows, near to the Vigna Oglietti, along the Vicolo of that name which had been incorporated into the cemetery in 1862. During the later expansion of the cemetery, all of these niches were destroyed to make way for modern cemetery buildings. (For the exact location of the site see O. Montenovesi *Guida del Verano*, Rome, 1925, p. 28 and above all, the plan numbered XXXII, 'Niches at Vicolo della Ranocchia'). Macpherson's age when he died (57), corresponds to the *Stati delle Anime* relating to his family. Those of the parish of S. Giacomo in Augusta for the year 1854, p. 46 state: 'Via dei Greci no. 44, Macpherson Roberto di Gio. Scotsman, aged 38'; the *Stato delle Anime* of the parish of S. Maria del Popolo for the year 1869, p. 76: 'Vicolo d'Alibert no. 12, Macpherson Roberto, di Giovanni, born in Edinburgh, photographer, 53 years of age etc.', *Stato delle Anime* of the parish of S. Maria del Popolo for the year 1871: 'Vicolo d'Alibert, no. 12, Macpherson Roberto, di Giovanni, born in Edinburgh, photographer, 55 years old, etc'. We assume from these entries that Macpherson was born in 1815 or at the latest 1816 and not in 1811 as indicated by various English historians. The discovery of his exact place of burial might have clarified this important point, but unfortunately, as recent research has shown, this has not been possible.

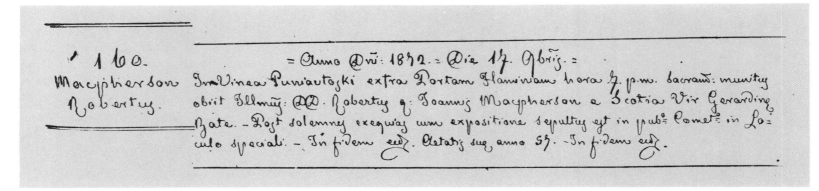

Robert Machperson's death certificate.

His obituary in the *British Journal of Photography* brings home the loss with the words: 'Few men will be missed more in the Eternal City than Robert Macpherson'[17].

His brave and loving window, Geraldine, was left with four children' two of whom were very young and rather sickly[18]. Poorly off after her husband's death, she tried as best as she could to be a dutiful mother. To support the family, she carried on Macpherson commercial dealings, this time selling not only his photographs, but also, when she had to, the negatives[19]. Other sources of income were English lessons, translation work and articles for British newspapers, particularly in the height of summer, when most journalists deserted Rome. But suddenly, while working on the memoirs of Anna Jameson in her house at number 22 Via del Vantaggio, she died from a heart attack. She was buried at Verano beside her beloved Robert[20]. The book on Anna Jameson was published after her death.

* * *

Photography had been astounding the world for some time, but only began to be a widespread phenomenon from the beginning of the 1850s, when technical developments allowed it to be used not just for portraits, but for taking pictures of works of art, buildings and views. In the wake of this new wave of enthusiasm, an old friend of Macpherson's from Edinburgh called Dr. Clark arrived in Rome with a camera. In fact Macpherson became fascinated by photography at just the time when his friend had been about to give it up because of technical problems and his basic lack of skill. He teamed up with Dr. Clark and the technical problems were soon sorted out[21].

17. See *The British Journal of Photography, op. cit.* p. 577.

18. At the time of Macpherson's death, his wife Geraldine had just recovered from an acute attack of rheumatism which had lasted for about a year. See post script by Mrs M. O. W. Oliphaunt to the *Memoirs of Anna Jameson* by G, Macpherson, published posthumously in London, 1878, p. XIII.

19. See the receipt given to Signora Cuccioni: 'Received from Signora Cuccioni 50 lire for sixteen small negatives. Geraldine Macpherson, 21 May 1874' (Becchetti's photographic archives).

20. See Harry Coghill, *Autobiography and Letters of M. O. W. Oliphaunt*, 1899, p. 58.

21. See Obituary, *op. cit*.

Receipt issued by Macpherson's widow, Geraldine, to Sig. Cuccioni on the sale of sixteen small negatives. 21 May 1874. (Coll. P. Becchetti, Rome).

Highly aware of the value and potential of this new art form, Macpherson threw himself completely into photography. He put aside his brushes for ever (although it is said that this was also due to deteriorating eyesight) and only ever returned to painting as a hobby[22].

Developments in the other visual arts played an important role in establishing the art of photography in the early days. A great tourist centre like Rome, where there was a constant demand for printed and painted reproductions of all its art treasures, had naturally attracted a lot of artists. Many of these felt so threatened by photography that they took it up themselves and often did quite well financially out of it. Among the more well-known and prolific of these were Gioacchino Altobelli, Pompeo Molins, James Anderson and Giacomo Caneva (ex-painters) and Oswald Ufer, Carlo Baldassare Simelli and Tommaso Cuccioni (who came from print making).

Robert Macpherson was an ex-painter, but he had also studied medicine. This useful combination of experience enabled him to reach a very high standad in record time. His understanding of chemistry allowed him to master all the techniques of the time, while his artistic background and talents helped him in the choice of subject and composition. By 1853, very soon after he had taken up the new art, he had already invented a new method of 'etching a photographic image onto a lithographic stone or plate, in such a way that, using the normal lithographic process, an indefinite number of copies could be produced.' He applied to the Ministry of Commerce, Fine Art, Industry, Agriculture and Public Works for a patent, and was granted one for six years[23].

22. See G. Macpherson, postscript by M. O. W. Oliphaunt, *op. cit.* p. XIII.

23. Sivio Negro was the first to publish details of this important document preserved in the State Records Office in Rome in his *Seconda Roma 1850-1870*, Hoepli, Milan, 1943, pp. 469-70.

So impressed was the Special Commission appointed to investigate the new procedure, (consisting of Father Angelo Secchi, Father G. Battista Piancioni and Professor Paolo Volpicelli), that having drawn up two detailed reports, they declared that they could give Macpherson patent rights as introducer, if not of downright inventor of the technique, 'the Commission having no other reports of anyone else practising this art in Italy'. The patent, which gave Macpherson exclusive rights to his new procedure, was signed by the Minister, Jacobini, on 6 August 1853 and reported in the *Giornale di Roma* on 9 August.

As well as well-earned fame among photographic circles in Rome, Macpherson's success with his invention also reassured him that he had made the right decision to give up painting. Clues to his state of mind after this early success can be found in a letter written by William Story to a mutual friend, James Russell Lowell, on 10 August 1853. Having just finished a statue of his father, Story writes that he is just about to send a photograph of it to his mother, and continues: 'This reminds me that Mac has just received a patent from the Papal Government for his new invention, which means that he can now make lithographs and prints from his photographs. The process has yet to be perfected, but has already proved a great success. The prints are so good that the Government gave him the patent immediately after examining some examples. This has given Mac a real boost, and he says he's going to grow his hair and beard another six inches!'[24]

The invention also brought Macpherson fame outside the Papal state. At the British Association for the Advancement of Science in Glasgow, in 1855, a lecture was given by Professor A. C. Ramsey, in which he described Macpherson's idea and showed those present examples of the prints obtained by this process. Shortly afterwards this lecture was transcribed in the Association's[25] journal and also appeared in Italian in the magazine *Nuovo Cimento*[26].

As Macpherson had become involved in photography quite late in life, he never made professional use of the early daguerrotypes and *calotipia* which were already being superceded by new techniques by the early 1850s. We know that in his earliest work he used albumin on glass, while by 1856 he had adopted the process based on a mixture of the chemicals collodion and albumin, as recommended by J. M. Taupenot in September 1855. This slow-drying process was particularly suitable for taking photographs indoors, where a long exposure time was necessary. At a meeting of the Photographic Society of Scotland in 1862, Macpherson explained that he used this process because years of experience had proved it the best for subjects requiring a long exposure. A distant panorama in good light would need an exposure time of five minutes, and closer subjects about 10-20 minutes, while in dark sculpture galleries exposures of two hours or even over two days were sometimes necessary in order to obtain a good negative[27]. Talking about his photo-lithographic process, he revealed that he had initially been reluctant to work on it – not because he thought it wouldn't work, but simply because lithographic stones and other materials were hard to come by in Rome, as were lithographers capable of such precision work[28].

Macpherson had only been a photographer for a few years, but his proven ability had already earned him a place among the circle of established photographers which included Giacomo

24. See G. R. Hudson, *Browning to his American Friends: Letters 1841-90*, 1965, p. 271.
25. See British Association for the Advancement of Science, Glasgow, Sept. 1855, pp. 69-70.
26. See *Nuovo Cimento* vol. II, 1855, pp. 278-281.
27. See *The Photographic Journal*, 15 Dec. 1862, p. 184.
28. *Ibidem.*

Caneva, James Anderson, Pietro Dovizielli, Tommaso Cuccioni and Luswergh. Official recognition came in 1856, when one of his prints was sent to the Academy of Sciences in Paris by Prof. Paolo Volpicelli on behalf of the Papal Government, to demonstrate the degree of skill and quality that photography had achieved in Rome. The print, of the famous *Laocöon* group, was praised far outside the rather narrow circle of expert photographers[29].

When the Architectural Photographic Association was founded in London in 1857, Macpherson began to exhibit his work at their annual shows. At the second show he exhibited 120 of his views[30]. People admired his photographs for their beautiful *chiaroscuro*, remarkable half-tones and richness of detail. This praise was somewhat dampened, however, by a very critical review in *The Photographic News*[31]. Among other faults, the author accused him of using a poor quality lens which distorted the sense of what he called '*gravità*', by which he probably meant perspective. His images were also said to lack the mathematical precision expected of architectural photographs. We can only conclude, as Gernsheim did when he wrote about this episode, that 'Philistines existed 100 years ago, just as they do now'[32].'

At the fourth show, in 1861, Macpherson exhibited fewer photographs, including those of the Vatican sculptures. The following year he exhibited over 400 views, which were well-received by the critics. One review said: 'the subjects have been selected with excellent taste and executed with skill and talent. The collector can find among them anything in Rome he desires, from the Colosseum to a cameo. The photographs of the best of the Vatican and Campidoglio sculptures were taken *in situ*, for which Macpherson had to obtain special permission. They are the first photographs ever taken of many of these magnificient works of art, which have always been the source of admiration and despair for artists[33].' Strangely enough, Macpherson did not take part in any other shows such as the international exhibitions held alternately in Paris, London and Dublin, in which many Roman photographers appeared on behalf of the Papal state.

It was the publication of the catalogue *Vatican Sculptures* which brought Macpherson the greatest fame as a photographer[34]. This slim volume, published in England in 1863, when he finished his work in the museums, is not only a collection of photographs, but also an excellent guide to the most important sculptures to be found there. Macpherson's education is clearly evident in the brief notes on the history and artistic merits of each work which introduce the photographs. In the introduction he recalls how, over his long period of residency in Rome, visits to the museums with famous artists and archaelogists had reawoken his interest in these great masterpieces. The discussions which must have taken place were obviously a precious source of information to him. And so, he says, he thought it would be useful to accompany each

29. A photograph by Luswergh was also sent. See *La Lumiere*, VI, no. 6, Feb. 1856 and M. Miraglia, Macpherson and Luswergh in *Fotografia Italiana dell'Ottocento*, Florence, 1979, pp. 162-163.

30. For more information on Macpherson's participation in the various exhibitions, see *Building News* 24 Dec. 1858; *Architectural Photographic Association Catalogue of the Second Annual Exhibition of English and Foreign Photographs*, 1861, pp. 16-17; *The Athenaeum* Aug. 1862; *The Photographic Journal*, 15 Dec. 1862 p. 184. Sincere thanks to Paolo Costantini for information about these shows.

31. 24 Dec. 1858, pp. 186-7.

32. See H. Gernsheim, *Robert Macpherson* in *Ferrania*, Milan, A. VIII, no. 10, Oct. 1954, p. 3.

33. See *The Athenaeum*, 9 August 1862, p. 181.

34. See R. Macpherson, *Vatican Sculptures, selected and arranged in the order in which they are found in the Galleries, briefly explained*, Chapman and Hall, Piccadilly, 1863. The second edition of the guide was published after his death in 1873.

VATICAN SCULPTURES,

SELECTED, AND ARRANGED

IN THE ORDER IN WHICH THEY ARE FOUND
IN THE GALLERIES,

BRIEFLY EXPLAINED BY

ROBERT MACPHERSON,

ROME.

"To speak suitably, and with real advantage to one's self and
others, of works of art, can properly be done only in their
presence. *All* depends on the sight of the object. On this it
depends whether the words by which we hope to elucidate the
Work produce the clearest impression, or none at all."—GOETHE.

LONDON:
CHAPMAN & HALL, 193 PICCADILLY.
1863.

[THE RIGHT OF TRANSLATION IS RESERVED.]

Title page of Vatican Sculptures. *London 1863.*
(Coll. P. Becchetti, Rome).

photograph with some concise notes taken from the works of people like Ennio Quirino Visconti, J. Joachim Winckelmann and, in particular, his compatriate, John Flaxman. Even more remarkable were the small woodcuts of the photographs, by his talented wife, Geraldine, which helped to clarify specific points. The words of Goethe in the preface are indicative of Macpherson's approach: 'To speak suitably, and with real advantage to oneself and others, of works of art, can properly be done only in their presence. *All* depends on the sight of the subject.'

Elsewhere in the introduction Macpherson made a very interesting statement about his profession: 'Photography has been my occupation for the last 12 years[35]. Although I started almost by accident, I soon found it all so interesting that I have remained a photographer until today, without realising that in doing so I have completely abandoned art to the point of losing the right to call myself an artist.' These words are not without a certain regret. Macpherson had not yet understood that, if he had lost his right to one title, he had gained another – that of 'artist of the lens.'

Macpherson's long argument with John Murray tells us more about his complex personality. It also teaches us something about the criteria used by the editors of certain guidebooks to select their lists of recommended shops or artists. One of the most famous English guidebooks to Rome for half of the nineteenth century was *Murray's Handbook*. Few English-speaking visitors to

35. He began taking photographs in 1851, as has been confirmed by other sources.

32

Rome would be without this guide, which was updated in many editions throughout the century to keep up with developments in the city. To help tourists find their way around in a strange city, there was also a special supplement called the *Handbook for Travellers* which was filled with information on museum timetables, addresses of language teachers, chemists, homeopathic doctors, hotels, restaurants, all kinds of shops and, seeing as photography was becoming more widespread, the names of photographers and of shops selling photographs. This handbook was the root of a bitter and polemic argument which even found its way into the pages of the London newspaper, *The Athenaeum*, in 1867[36].

Robert Macpherson's anger was first roused by certain comments about him in the new 1867 edition of *Murray's*. Feeling rather offended, he wrote a polite letter to the publisher, John Murray, requesting an explanation:

'To Mr. John Murray.

12, Vicolo d'Alibert, Rome. March 1867.

Dear Sir, – I don't for a moment suppose that it is of any importance to the world to know where I come from, but it is of importance to *me* that I should not be suspected of being an imposter, passing myself off as belonging to another part of the world instead of my own, which is England, or, to be more precise, Scotland. The people employed to work for your handbook are supposed, by many, to get their information from the horse's mouth and, therefore, since you have named me courteously for so many years in the *Handbook for Rome* as a countryman of yours, and this year in the edition which has just come out you call me a Canadian, it looks as if I told your servants that I was so, – which being the reverse of the truth, I request that you will contradict this statement in *The Times* and in *The Athenaeum*. I make this request in the spirit of friendliness, as I think it would come better from you than from me. All the world knows who John Murray is; I have heard enough about you through friends such as Mr. Poole and Mr. Hepworth Dixon to be certain that you *personally* had nothing to do with that falsehood, in which I can see malice; and I cannot help but apply to you as the publisher and proprietor, as I am not legally supposed to know the originators of the statement nor the motives for making it. There is much discontent expressed in Rome with your Handbook; its defects are chiefly known to those who know Rome well. I am convinced that you do everything in your power to make it perfect; but I fear that you will find that many others beside myself will be troubling you.

I have the honour to remain, dear Sir, yours very sincerely, Robert Macpherson[37]'.

Murray replied that he did not understand the motive for the complaint. Describing Macpherson as a Canadian was certainly not defamatory, as in general Canadians were held in high esteem and some had recently been awarded honours by Queen Victoria. A public retraction would, he said, be simply ridiculous; he would correct the error in the next edition. But towards the end of the letter he seemed to hint at the possible elimination of Macpherson's name from the hand book altogether.

36. The letters in question were published as a group only twice, on 4 May and 1 June 1867. To clarify matters we have listed them in chronological order.

37. This obscure paper, of which only a few issues seem to have survived, came out every Tuesday, Thursday and Saturday, except in the Summer, and was published in French. The issue referred to is preserved in the archives of the Becchetti collection in Rome.

Macpherson was naturally insulted by these vague insinuations and wrote again to Murray, offering his own explanations for what had happened:

'To Mr. John Murray.

12 Vicolo d'Alibert, Rome. April 2. 1867.

Sir – On 6 of last month I addressed to you a kindly and civil communication, in accordance with a direct request in your Handbooks that errors therein might be pointed out to you; and I certainly had the right to expect a reply couched in terms of common courtesy. It is the manifest duty of a publisher who has undertaken the onerous and responsible office (self-imposed) of directing the travelling British public to make accuracy of information and equitable description his chief object, and gratefully to accept the rectification of unconscious, much more of wanton and malicious, errors. I am forced, however, by the undignified and unworthy tone of your note, to conclude that such is not your opinion. Of course I shall not suffer the misrepresentations in the *Handbook for Rome* to remain for three years uncorrected; and as you decline applying the requisite remedy, shall do it myself. Your plea of inadvertent error is untrue; there is no inadvertence whatsoever in the deliberate alteration of the text, which was satisfactory as it stood in former editions. The principle motive for the change you know as well as I do. It is, that I had ceased to respond to the importunate solicitations of your agent, and had suspended the annual contributions of photographs he exacted, and which he habitually described as being most acceptable to yourself. Nor will I leave unnoticed the capricious partiality and desire to gratify petty malice, which are well-understood here, and of which there are already in Rome alone too many just complaints. As my letter contained not a word against Canadians, your attributing to me unkind sentiments towards them which I never entertained was equally gratuitous and irrelevant. I simply desired you to correct a mistake confusing my identity, and calculated to be injurious to me on that account; but the last paragraph of your note contains the almost unequivocable statement that it is a condition of any mention whatsoever being made in your Handbook that you are to be permitted impunity of error, and that the burdensome demands made in your name by your agent are to be unconditionally complied with. Leave my name, then, unnoticed in future! I much prefer to throw myself unaided upon a very large number of friends and a discriminating public unbiassed by misdirection, and with whose kindness and appreciation long experience has rendered me perfectly satisfied.

I have the honour to remain, Sir, your most obedient servant, Robert Macpherson'.

The letter left Rome on 2 April and arrived in London on 8 April. Murray answered by return of post, with a letter that aggravated the matter still further. He admitted that he possessed some of Macpherson's photographs, but denied categorically thay they had been given with the purpose of obtaining a favourable review. Had this been the case, he said, he would have returned them immediately. All these arrangements were completely in the hands of the editor in Rome. As it appeared to him, the accusation of 'falsehood, petty malice, bribery and bias' had arisen solely because Macpherson had mistakenly been referred to as a Canadian.

On 20 April Macpherson wrote once again to the editor, accusing him of blackmail and stating his belief that only by complying with Murray's conditions would he succeed in getting a favourable entry. He ended: 'It is now too late to change the past. As far as I can see, it cannot be denied that a favourable or infavourable review in your so-called *Guide for Travellers* be the result of pure business dealings and not of information given in good trust.'

On 29 April Murray answered:

'To Mr. Robert Macpherson.

London, April 29.

Sir – I am certainly greatly surprised to hear from you that the six or seven photographs, now on their way back to Rome, given by you to the editor of the *Handbook for Rome*, for which, if you remember, *he offered payment*, were intended by you as a bribe, that is to say, as an inducement to place you in a higher position than you deserve as a Roman photographer. Yet in consequence of this you make a charge of systematic bribery and exaction against the *Handbooks for Travellers* and their publisher.

If there be such a system, it must be very clumsily carried out. *You* bribed, and instead of praise got very scurvy notice, by your own account, and finally, insult was added to injury by calling you a Canadian! After such a result I am not surprised that you desisted from attempts to bribe the *Handbook*, and the more widely you promulgate to the world the miserable story of your own want of success, the better I shall be pleased, as it will preserve others from falling into the delusion that praise or blame in the Handbook can be purchased by gift.

I am, Sir, yours &c. John Murray.'

John Murray also sent a letter to the editor of *The Athenaeum*, requesting publication, in which he explained that the task of selecting and classifying the names of shopkeepers, hotel owners and others in his Guide was not easy, and that those who considered themselves better than others were deluded.

As might be expected, Macpherson promptly wrote to the newspaper to reply to these new assertions:

'12 Vicolo d'Alibert, Rome. May 10, 1867.

Sir – In your number of May 4 appear the two concluding letters of a correspondence between Mr. John Murray and myself, which, standing alone, are calculated to convey to the public a false impression concerning the relations between us. I am sure I do not overrate your sense of justice in supposing that, having opened your columns to one party, you will permit the other to make known the whole facts of the case.

In Mr. Murray's *Handbook of Central Italy* of 1856, there appeared an unsolicited notice concerning me, of which the following is a part: 'Of recent years, photography has been very successfully applied in delineating the monuments of Ancient and Modern Rome. By far the finest are those made by our countryman, Mr. Macpherson, who lives at No. 4, Via de' Strozzi, where they may be obtained.'

Immediately after the publication of this, the agent of Mr. Murray in Rome, Mr. Pentland, with whom I had been unacquainted, introduced himself to me and indicated that I ought to signify my appreciation of the handsome notice I had received by sending to Mr. Murray, through him, some of my most valuable photographs. After repeated and importunate representations to this effect, I gave Mr. Pentland, on 15 June, 1856, 25 of my photographs.

I made an entry in my books of the number and subjects of the same, which would constitute legal evidence of the fact. No 'offer of payment' was made or hinted at, either then or on the occasion of subsequent donation.

In 1858, the *Handbook for Rome*, says: 'Mr. Macpherson, who was one of the first to introduce photography and lives at 192 Via Ripetta, where his work may be procured, has extended his labours to the monuments of other towns of the Roman States; his collection already includes 2000 subjects.' Shortly after this, Mr. Pentland renewed his demand for a contribution of photographic views, and my books contain, accordingly, the record of ten more I then gave him. But for the last time. The darker aspect of the whole business had become apparent and I told Mr. Pentland that he must expect nothing more.

The consequence was, that in the handbooks for 1862 and 1864, my name was crowded into the common catalogue succeeding the panegyrics on Mr. Pentland's more newly-favoured friends.

However unjust this might be, I did not complain of it. But in the edition for this year (1867), Mr. Murray has seen fit to substitute for the words, 'Our countryman, Mr. Macpherson', 'Mr. Macpherson, a *Canadian*... an excellent photographer of views or Rome &c.' I felt far from

Advertisement placed in the newspaper Arrivée des Étrangers à Rome, *6 October 1870. (Coll. P. Becchetti, Rome).*

'insulted', as Mr. Murray insinuated, at this; but, wishing to maintain my Scots identity before the world, opened with him the subsequent correspondence.

In Mr. Murray's letter he intimates that he has never received more than six of my photographs. Mr. Pentland ought to know what has become of the remainder. He received from me, from first to last, as nearly as I can estimate, not less than 60.

Robert Macpherson.'

No further letters were published in *The Atheneaeum* and it seems as if the matter was allowed to drop. This may have been partly to do with tiredness, but Macpherson was a stubborn man, who was convinced he was in the right, and he still felt very bitter.

There is more than a trace of the animosity between him and Murray in the *Vatican Sculptures* catalogue published on 1 March 1868. At the bottom of a page, in bold type, is printed the following warning: 'Visitors travelling with Murray's Handbook are informed that a correspondence with Mr. Murray, on the subject of misrepresentations contained in the *Handbook for Rome*, has been printed; copies of which may be had on application to Mr. Macpherson'.

And in 1870, he also placed an advertisement in the journal *Arrivée des étrangers a Rome*, which includes the statement: 'NB: Visitors travelling with Murray's Handbook will no longer find Robert Macpherson's name in its pages. The explanation of which will be found in a correspondence published a short time ago in the London *Athenaeum*. A printed copy of this correspondence can be obtained *gratis* on application to Mr. Macpherson'. It has so far been impossible to trace this leaflet, but it seems certain into have contained additional comments on the matter. We do know for sure that, from the eighth edition of *Murray's Handbook* (after 1867), Robert Macpherson's name was eliminated from its pages.

By the beginning of the 1870s Robert Macpherson was well established and business was going excellently. However, rapid changes were afoot in the photographic world - both on account of strong competition and also the dramatic changes going on in Rome. Macpherson's photographs may have been aesthetically beautiful, but they no longer gave visitors a true picture of Rome. Macpherson also had to try to adapt himself to the times by producing a quality product at a more accessible price, and the discovery of a more economical and practical working procedure by Ernest Edwards in England helped him to cut his production costs successfully. Macpherson immediately filed a request for property rights to this new typographic process, informing the Papal Ministry of Commerce that the inventor, Ernest Edwards, had already been granted patents by the Queen of England, the Emperor of France and the King of Belgium.

The request, which was presented jointly by Macpherson and Edwards, has been preserved in the State Records Office in Rome[38]. It resulted in a detailed report drawn up by Professor Ratti, whom the Government had charged with investigating the legitimacy of the request. The report states: 'I asked Mr. Macpherson to explain the exact amounts of the various chemicals used, and the degree of caution necessary throughout the process. In the end I was convinced that even someone completely ignorant of the method could have the opportunity to achieve results like those of Mr. Edwards, just by following the instructions. Mr. Macpherson has fulfilled my request – he has explained Mr. Edwards' methods briefly and precisely and has sought the collaboration of the inventor himself. I have written it all down and include it in the enclosed parcel labelled 'Description of Mr. Edwards' photo-typographic method, as explained by Mr. Macpherson.' I then visited Mr. Macpherson's studio and established that it was sufficiently well-equipped to carry out production on a large scale. Although the process resembles photo-lithography in many ways, different chemicals are used and the lithographic press is replaced by a typographic one. For these reasons I am of the opinion that Mr. Macpherson should be granted rights of ownership. 27 August 1870.'

But another member of the Commission nominated to investigate the request was of the opposite opinion. According to Mr. Grifi, Edwards' invention was too similar to photo-lithography, and they could not be granted rights of ownership because of the risk of disputes with other candidates such as Danesi, Rossi, Mang, Ufer, Martorelli and others. Professor Ratti replied that the main difference from all in the other different processes was the typographic press, which made the whole process so much simpler.

Macpherson was therefore granted his license. It was published in the *Giornale di Roma* on September 15 1870, along with all the official records of the Ministry of Commerce:

'Inventions and discoveries for which property rights have been granted in accordance with the Decree of September 3, 1833: The use of the typographic press for the state for six years and already had the rights from other governments.' There is also a letter from Macpherson dated September 15, 1870, in which he promises to pay the Papal state the sum of 161.25 lire 'in settlement of the tax applied to the granting of property rights for six years, in accordance with the Ministerial Decree of 14 September 1870, no. 6913[39], clause 3a.'

Macpherson's work was given some indirect publicity in 1871 by Robert Burn. His latest book, *Rome and Campagna*[40], was illustrated with prints, about 40 of which were taken from Macpherson's photographs. As *The Athenaeum* stressed, one of the most remarkable aspects of the book were these woodcuts taken from Macpherson's photographs and executed with great skill by the late artist Orlando Jewitt[41].

Work by Robert Macpherson which is not in any of the various public and private collections is recorded in the numerous catalogues which he published throughout the 20 years of his career. The first catalogue dates from 1858 and includes 163 pictures, while the next, which came out in 1860, contains 19. In August 1863, when his guide to the Vatican Museum sculptures was published, Macpherson also had his entire photographic catalogue printed. This long list

38. State Archives, Rome, Ministry of Commerce, envelope 421.

39. *Ibidem*.

40. See Robert Burn, *Rome and Campagna, An Historical and Topographical Description of the Sites, Buildings and Neighbourhood of Ancient Rome*, Cambridge London, 1871, pp. LXXXIII, 483.

41. *The Athenaeum*, 21 Jan, 1871. Some of these prints were to be used by T. H. Dyer in his book, *The City of Rome*, 1893.

comprises 305 photographs taken not only in Rome and its surroundings, but also further afield in Lazio and Umbria. On 1 March 1868 he published a list of 128 photographs of the sculptures in the Vatican Museums, while in 1871, to mark the completion of his project in the Capitoline Museum, a catalogue describing the 278 photographs was brought out. His last catalogue, a general one of 420 views, was published at the same time. This catalogue contained new views of Ancona, Capri, Gubbio and Ostia Antica, but many of the older views of the outskirts of Rome, which had been included in the last catalogue, were excluded. Of the 420 numbers, 63 are empty[42]. A further undated catalogue, which was probably published around 1865, includes 135 photographs of prints taken from famous pictures. Another catalogue is known about, but is as yet untraceable. An advert placed in a Roman newspaper on 6 Oct 1870 describes 'a complete collection of the Christian sarcophagi in the Lateran Museum'[43].

Some other views of Rome and its surroundings have come to light. Most of these are rather different from those in the catalogues – they are of a different size and are stamped and numbered differently, which makes it possible that they might be part of another collection.

There are also the pictures which Macpherson was commissioned to take for special occasions – such as to record the progress of work on the bridge at S. Anatolia or on the Velletri railway line[44].

Robert Macpherson's photographic production was not particularly prolific. An examination of the inventories reveals only about 1000 photographs over many years of activity. His somewhat limited activity is illustrated particularly clearly in the catalogue of views. With the exception of Rome, there are very few views of other aesthetically interesting cities in the area, such as Orvieto, Perugia and Gubbio. The way he worked was to choose his subjects carefully, thus reducing his activity to the absolute minimum.

Most of Macpherson's photographs are quite large. The views are usually rectangular, but sometimes, when the peripheral details of the image are unimportant, he makes very effective use of the oval format[45]. This concentrates the eye of the viewer on the centre of the picture. His striking way of framing a view enabled Macpherson to create images which are, at times, almost surreal. They are not just aesthetically interesting; the way in which the horizontal and vertical aspects of the subject are exploited almost amounts to a new photographic language. In his

42. In the Catalogue of 1873 besides Rome, there are three views of Anzio, seven of Assisi, one of Borghetto, one of Bracciano, three of the Roman countryside, one of Caprarola, one of Castel Madama, four of Civitavecchia, two of Cori, two of Fossanova, five of Frascati, one of Nepi, three of Nettuno, two of Ninfa, three of Norcia, three of Narni, three of Orvieto, two of Paestum, one of the Pontine Paludi, six of Perugia, one of Ponte Lucano, two of Sermoneta, five of Spoleto, four of Subiaco, one of Terni; three of Terracina, sixteen of Tivoli, two of Tuscania, four of Velletri, and two of Vicovaro. In the 1871 catalogue the views of Anzio, one of Assisi, those of Castel Madama, Civitavecchia, Frascati, Nettuno, one of Ninfa, those of Norcia, one of Narni, two of Orvieto, those of Paestum, one of Spoleto, one of Terracina, two of Tivoli and one of Velletri are not included, while three views of Ancona, two of Ariccia, one of Capri, one of Gubbio, two of Nemi and four of Ostia Antica have been added.

43. See *Arrivée des Étrangers à Rome, op. cit.*

44. The pictures in question, which are reproduced in this book, come from the Luigi Poletti Library in Modena. Once again, I would like to thank Dr. Rossella Ruggeri, Director of the Library, for granting us permission to publish then.

45. Of many of the views both rectangular and oval versions exist. Worthy of note are: the view of the cascades at Marmore, the Rocca Pia at Tivoli, the view across Rome from Caecilia Metella and the view of the Via Appia from the Church of S. Sebastiano. Macpherson would often take new versions of some of the views in the catalogues, as if he were not satisfied with them, but the inventory numbers remained the same.

views, especially, the combination of careful study and composition and the spontaneous play of light and shadow results in images which have real poetic quality.

Visitors to Rome found instilled in his photographs all that had captured their imagination during their stay in the city – the sunshine, the clear air, the presence of the ruins and all the evidence of the splendours of the past. His strong visual powers never failed to evoke an unforgettable sense of romance and history. Tourists wanted a photograph which could somehow capture all that they had felt when looking at a particular view or monument – an image which would bring flooding back at a glance some of their experiences in those places.

Having been both a painter and a tourist in Rome, Robert Macpherson knew these feelings well and somehow managed to pin them down with his lens. Pictures such as those of the Temple of the 'Tosse' at Tivoli, the Temple of Hercules in Cori, the Rocca dei Borgia in Nepi, his view across Rome from the Palatine to the Circus Maximus, or of the Ponte Felice near Civita Castellana all bear witness to his creativity with the camera.

Macpherson loved Rome deeply, and was a skilful, observant and sensitive interpeter of all the city's ever-changing aspects throughout the year. He took pictures of the famous fountains in the Piazza della Bocca della Verità (Bizzaccheri) and the Piazza Barberini (Bernini) in both summer and winter, because, like a 'real Roman', he knew that they took on completely different appearances and qualities with the change in light. He evokes all the atmosphere and emotions conjured up by the extraordinary pattern of anachronisms and contrasts which made up the Rome of that time. And through that complex, contradictory and silent city, which consisted almost entirely of monuments, villas and gardens, the Tiber ran its unrestricted course, with the foundations of ancient houses sunk deep into its muddy waters. It is in these views of the river – sometimes wild, sometimes majestic – that Macpherson's powers of observation and artistic synthesis are seen at their best.

As well as one of the greatest architectural photographers (as Gernsheim has rightly claimed)[46], Robert Macpherson was also the last real poet of Papal Rome. His photographs have preserved the appearance of a city suspended between its past and future. Very soon, after 20 September 1870, Rome's new role as the capital of Italy was to transform it completely, banishing for ever much of its devastating and ancient charm.

Piero Becchetti

46. See H. Gernsheim, *Robert Macpherson op. cit.*

BIBLIOGRAPHY

Archival sources:

Archivio del Vicariato di Rome.
    Stato delle Anime della parrocchia di S.Maria del Popolo, 1867-1872.
    Stato delle Anime della parrocchia di S. Giacomo in Augusta, 1865-1866.
    Liber XIX mortuorum de S. Mariae de Populo Urbis, anno 1872.

Archivio di Stato, Rome.
    Fondo Ministero del Commercio, 1859 and 1870.
    Fondo del Buon Governo, Police Records. List of photographers and photography shops and studios in Rome, about 1866.

Archivio Cartaceo IV Ripartizione, registry office form for Geraldine Macpherson.

Records of burials at the Verano Cemetery, 1872 and 1878.

Archives of the Becchetti photographic Collection, Rome. Receipt issued by Geraldine Macpherson on selling some negatives, 1875.

Published sources:

H. Le Grice, *Walks through the studii of the sculptors at Rome,* Rome, 1841, p. 280.

The Roman Advertiser, Rome, 24 Oct. 1846, 28 Oct. 1848, 30 Dec. 1848.

Il Giornale di Roma, Rome, 9 Aug. 1853.

Nuovo Cimento, Florence, 1855.

Almanacco romano, Rome, 1855.

British Association for Advancement of Science, Glasgow, Sept. 1855.

La Lumiére, A. VI, 9 Feb. 1856.

The handbook for travellers, in *Handbook of Rome and its environs,* J. Murray, London, 1856, 1858, 1862, 1864, 1867, 1867 second edition.

Macpherson's photographs, Rome, 1858.

The Building News, 24 Dec. 1858.

The Photographic News, Feb. 1860.

Macpherson's photographs, Rome, undated, about 1860.

Architectural Photographic Association, catalogue, second annual exib. 1861.

The Athenaeum, 9.8.1862; 4.5.1867 and 1.6.1867.

Macpherson's photographs, Rome, August 1863.

R. Macpherson, *Vatican sculptures,* Piccadilly, 1863.

The Photographic Journal, 15 Dec. 1862.

Macpherson's photographs of celebrated pictures mostly taken from the best engravings. Rome, 1865.

Macpherson's Vatican sculptures, 1 March 1868.

C. MacKenzie, *A trip to Rome,* 1869.

Arrivée des étrangers à Rome. 6 October, 1870.

Giornale di Roma, 15 Sep. 1870.

Macpherson's photographs, Dec. 1871.

Macpherson's sculptures of the Capitol, 287 in all, Rome, Dec. 1871.

R. Burn, *Rome and Campagna,* Cambridge, 1871.

Guida Monaci per la Città di Roma, 1871-1876.

The British Journal of Photography, London, 6 Dec. 1872.

R. Macpherson, *Vatican Sculptures,* second edition, Calzone, Rome, 1873.

J.E. Freeman, *Gatherings from an artist's portfolio,* New York, 1877.

G. Macpherson, *Memoirs of Anna Jameson,* London, 1878.

J.E. Freeman, *Gatherings from an artist's portfolio in Rome,* Boston, 1883.

H. Coghill, *Autobiography and letters of Mrs. M.O. Oliphant,* 1899.

D. Angeli, *Cronache del Caffè Greco,* Milan, 1939.

S. Negro, *Seconda Roma,* Hoepli, Milan, 1943, pp. 399, 469-470.

Masterpieces of victorian photography 1840-1900, from Gernsheim collection, London, 1951.

H. and A. Gernsheim, *Robert Macpherson,* in *Ferrania,* Milan, A.VIII, Oct. 1954.

Exhibition of photographs from the Gernsheim collection arranged by the British Council in Rome, Florence, Bologna and Milan in 1954.

H. and A. Gernsheim, *The history of photography,* 'Oxford, 1955, pp. 221-223.

H. Gernsheim, *Creative photography aesthetic trends 1839-1960;* London, 1962.

G.R. Hudson, *Browning to his american friends: letters 1851-1890,* 1965.

P. Becchetti, *Robert Macpherson,* in *Roma cento anni fa nelle fotografie del tempo,* catalogue, Rome, 1971, pp. 16-17 and 81-82.

M. Wynne, *Fesch paintings in the National Gallery of Ireland, Gazette des Beaux Arts,* Jan. 1977.

P. Becchetti, *Robert Macpherson,* in *Rome in Early Photographs. The age of Pius IX 1846-1878. From Roman and Danish collections. Copenaghen, 1977.*

P. Becchetti, Fotografi e fotografia in Italia 1839-1880. Quasar, Rome, 1978.

M. Miraglia, Macpherson Robert, in *Fotografia italiana dell'800,* Florence, 1979.

W.M. Watson, *Images of Italy, photography in the Nineteenth Century Mount* Holyoke College of Art Museum, South Hadley, 1980.

R. Pare, *Photography and Architecture 1839-1939,* 1982.

P. Becchetti, *La fotografia a Roma dalle origini al 1915,* Editore Colombo, Rome, 1983, pp. 22, 294, 303, 319-320, 347, illus. p. 82, 85, 86, 107.

R. McKenzie, *The cradle and grave of empires: Robert Macpherson and the photography of nineteenth century Rome,* in *The photographic collector,* London, 1983, Vol. 4, n. 2.

R. Elwail, *Architectural photographic association* in *The photographic collector,* London, 1985, vol. 5, n. 2.

A.A.V.V., *Pittori fotografi a Roma 1845-1870,* Rome, 1987.

MACPHERSON'S
PHOTOGRAPHS
ROME.
192. Via di Ripetta

Title page of one of Macpherson's albums of photographs.

MACPHERSON'S
PHOTOGRAPHS
ROME.

192. Via di Ripetta. 1858.

N.°

1. Arch of Constantine — South façade.
2. Arch of Constantine — North façade.
3. Arch of Constantine — North façade, including the Meta Sudans, and portion of the Convent of St. Bonaventura.
4. The fountain of Trevi.
5. A portion of the Forum of Nerva, sometimes called Temple of Pallas.
6. Another view of the same, taking in the figure of Minerva in the centre.
7. Columns of the Forum of Nerva, and the Arch called « L'Arco dei Pantani ».
8. The three Columns at the foot of the Capitol, formerly styled the Temple of Jupiter Tonans, and the Arch of Septimius Severus.
9. The eight Columns at the foot of the Capitol, formerly styled the Temple of Concord, and now the Temple of Vespasian or Temple of Saturn.
10. A view of the same in extreme profile, including a portion of the Basilica of Constantine, Phoca's Column, and the Arch of Titus.
11. The same Temple, seen from one side.
12. Temple of Venus and Rome with distant view of the Roman Forum; taken from the Coliseum.
13. Excavations of the Julian Basilica, including a view of the various Temples in the Forum, with the Arch of Titus and Alban mount in the distance.
14. Base of the Column in the Forum of Trajan.
15. Forum Romanum, looking towards the Capitol.
16. Forum Romanum — General view taken from the Clivus Capitolinus and including the principal Temples in the Forum, and the Arch of Titus.
17. Temple of Vesta and House of Rienzi.
18. Temple of Vesta and the Fountain, taken in winter.
19. Temple of Vesta and the Fountain, taken in summer.
20. Forum of Trajan.
21. Side view of the Temple dedicated to Antoninus and Faustina, Roman Forum.
22. View of the « Ponte Rotto » with the new Suspension bridge.
23. Façade of the Church of St. John Lateran.
24. Ruin called the Temple of Minerva Medica.
25. The Garden-front of the Villa Medici, built from the design of Michael-Angelo — on the Pincian Hill.
26. The Porta Maggiore, and Tomb of the Baker.
27. Arch of Titus, Roman Forum.
28. Basrelief in the interior of the Arch of Titus, representing the procession of the seven-branched Clandlestick.
29. Equestrian bronze Statue of Marcus Aurelius, standing in the square of the Capitol.
30. The Coliseum with Meta Sudans and portion of the Via Sacra.
31. The Coliseum with view of the Latin mountains, and the Church of St. John Lateran.
32. The Coliseum on a smaller scale, with distant Latin and Alban mountains, and Church of St. John Lateran.
33. Portion of the interior wall of the Coliseum.
34. The Castle and bridge of St. Angelo with the Vatican in the distance.
35. The Castle St. Angelo on a larger scale.
36. The Garden in the Vatican styled « della Pigna » containing the marble base of a Column dedicated to Antoninus; architecture of Bramante.
37. Bas-relief representing funereal games, being one side of the Base of the Antonine Column, in the Garden of the Vatican.
38. Bas-relief on the other side of the base of the Antonine Column, representing the Apotheosis of Antoninus and Faustina.
39. Church of Santa Pudenziana, the Titular Church of Cardinal Wiseman.
40. Fountain of the piazza Barberini, taken in winter.
41. Basilica of Costantine, formerly called the Temple of Peace; in the Forum.
42. Interior in the Vatican, styled the Hall of the Philosophers.
43. Church of Santa Maria Maggiore.
44.
45. Tomb of Cecilia Metella, with distant view of Rome.
46. Tomb of Cecilia Metella, and view of the Via Appia from the Church of St. Sebastian.

47. Temple of Fortuna Virilis, and house of Rienzi.
48. Cloisters of St. Paul's, the Basilica out-side the walls of Rome.
49.
50. Base of the Obelisk and Fountain in the Piazza Navona.
51. Church of the Trinità de' Monti.
52. Front of a Gothic Church at Vicovaro, near Tivoli.
53. Church of Santa Maria in Cosmedin; called the « Bocca della Verità ».
54. Arch of the Consul Dolabella on the Celian Hill.
55. View of the Capitoline Hill, from the foot of the Aventine.
56. View of the Aventine from the Tarpean Rock.
57. Piazza of St. Peter's.
58. St. Peter's from the Janiculum Hill.
59. St. Peter's with the Inquisition.
60.

61.

62. Phoca's Column, Temple of Vespasian, Tabularium, etc.
63. Group of Stone pines in the Villa Doria.
64. Cypresses planted by Michael-Angelo in the Cloisters of Santa Maria degli Angeli.
65. Colossal Head of the Emperor Domitian, in the Vatican Museum.
66. Arch of Septimius Severus, in the Roman Forum.
67. View of the Cloaca Massima, Temple of Vesta, Church of the « Bocca della Verità », etc.
68. The three Columns, formerly called the Temple of Jupiter Stator, and now styled Minerva Chalcidica, with the Temples of Peace, Antoninus and Faustina, etc. in the Roman Forum.
69. View of the Lake in the Villa Doria.
70. House of Lucrezia Borgia near the Church of San Pietro in Vincula.
71. A painting by Enghert representing an episode in Sicilian history viz : the arrest of the family of Manfred by order of Charles d'Anjou.
72. Bas-relief by Gibson, the Hours leading forth the horses of the Sun.
73. Bas-relief by Gibson, Phaeton guiding the Chariot and horses of the Sun.
74. Last Judgement in the Sixtine Chapel, taken from an unpublished drawing after Michael-Angelo.
75. The Apollo Belvedere.
76. Arch of the Goldsmiths, sometimes called the little Arch of Septimius Severus, in the Forum Boarium.
77. The Statue of Livia, also called the Pudicitia, in profile, in the Braccio nuovo, Vatican Museum.
78. The Sleeping Ariadne, formerly called the Cleopatra; Hall of the Philosophers. Vatican.
79. Guido painting Beatrice Cenci in prison the day preceding her execution. From a painting by Ratti.
80. The Bull-Slayer; Hall of the Animals. Vatican.
81. The Laocoon; Vatican Museum.
82. The Nile and its tributaries. Vatican.
83. The Roman Campagna near the Frascati Railway.
84. View of Tombs on the Via Appia.
85. Marriage of Cupid and Psyche.
86. Venus — front view.
87. Venus — in profile.
88. Venus — back view. } GIBSON.
89. Phoca's Column, excavated to the base.
90. Front view of the Livia of the Vatican, commonly called the Pudicitia.
91. The three Columns in the Forum, formerly called the Temple of Jupiter Stator, and now the Temple to Minerva Calcidica.
92. The same Temple as n.° 91 from the other side.
93. Ulysses, by Macdonald.
94. The Piazza del Popolo, looking from the Corso.
95. The Arch of Septimius Severus on a smaller scale than the same subject n.° 66.
96.
97. The Statue of Moses, by Michael-Angelo in the Church of San Pietro in Vincula.

98. The Fountain of the Doge, in the Cortile of the Venetian Palace.
99. " Sabrina " from Milton's " Comus " by Cardwell.
100. View of the Alban Mountains from the Church of San Pietro in Montorio.
101. View on the Campagna 4 miles from the Lateran gate, on the Naples road.
102. View of the Acqueduct — Acqua Claudia.
103. Large view of the Claudian Acqueduct.
104. Easter Benediction at St. Peter's.
105. Cupid and the Nymphs — From a painting by Wider.
106. The Indian, by Crawford.
107. Church of « Capo-Croce ». Near Frascati.
108. Porta Furba, Frascati road.
109. View over Rome from the Janiculum.
110. Palace of the Cesars on the Palatine.
111. Arch of Septimius Severus looking from the Forum.
112. Arch of Janus Quadrifrons.
113. Interior of the Sibyl's Temple at Tivoli.
114. Temple of the Sibyl. Tivoli.
115. — on a larger scale.
116. — seen from the bridge.
117. — — from the opposite side of the Ravine.
118. Large Waterfall.
119. Cascatelle at the Villa of Mecenas.
120. Temple styled « Della Tosse ».
121. Cypresses in Villa D'Este.
122. The Ravine with Temple of the Sibyl and Grotte of Neptune.
123. Castle of Tivoli.
124. Acqueduct near Castel Madama.
125. Ponte Lugano — with the Tomb of Plautius.
126. The Valley of the Anio with the upper and lower Cascatelle, Mecenas's Villa and distant Campagna.
127. Palazzo Altoviti on the Tiber.
128. Pyramid of Caius Cestius, and the English burying ground.
129. Madonna and Child, from the original painting by Sasso-Ferrato.
130. Cathedral of Orvieto.
131. Central doorway of the same.
132. Side-door on the left with bas-reliefs.
133. Bas-reliefs illustrative of the history of Christ.
134. Bas-relief of the « Last Judgement », « Paradiso and Hell ».
135. Etruscan gateway at Perugia.
136. Fountain in the Piazza del Duomo at Perugia.
137. Church of San Bernardino. Perugia.
138.
139. Falls of Terni.
140. View of the Valley and town of Narni.
141. Royal Palace at Caprarola.
142. Façade of the Church of Santa Maria at Toscanella.
143. Principal doorway of the above.
144. Group from a fresco by Luca Signorelli at Orvieto.
145.
146. Piazza del Popolo looking south.
147.
148. Horses of the Capitol from the Palazzo Caffarelli.
149. View over Rome from the Palatine Hill.
150. Bas-relief of the Biga — Arch of Titus.
151. Window in the House of Lucrezia Borgia.
152. Piazza and Fountain of the Tartarughe.
153. Tomb of Cecilia Metella, from the Road, « Via Appia ».
154. The Cloaca Maxima.
155. Valley of Egeria.
156. Elms in the Valley of Egeria.
157. Grotto of Egeria.
158. Porta San Lorenzo.
159. Statue of Minerva Medica.
160. Statue of Demosthenes.
161. Statue of Silenus holding Bacchus.
162. Statue of the Livia of the « Braccio nuovo ».
163. The Theatre of Marcellus, from the Piazza Montanara.

Catalogue of Macpherson's photographs. (Private collection).

ROME - Vicolo d'Alibert 12.

The Photographs in this List are of one uniform price namely 3 francs each.

The Stanze of Raphael in the Vatican.

1. Costantine addressing his soldiers, and seeing the Labarum.
2. The Battle at the « Pons Milvius » and victory of Constantine.
3. The Baptism of Constantine by St. Sylvester.
4. The donation of the city of Rome to St. Sylvester.
5. The expulsion of Heliodorus from the temple.
6. The miracle of Bolsena.
7. The meeting of Pope Leo II. and Attila, Attila terrified by SS. Peter and Paul.
8. St. Peter delivered by an Angel from prison.
9. Theology.
10. Philosophy.
11. Poetry.
12. Justice.
13. The dispute of the Sacrament.
14. The school of Athens.
15. Mount Parnassus, Apollo, and the Muses.
16. Jurisprudence.
17. Justification of Leo III, Leo clearing himself by oath before Charlemagne.
18. The coronation of Charlemagne by Leo the third.
19. The « Incendio del Borgo ».
20. The defeat of the Saracens at Ostia, Pontificate of Leo IV.

Also the Loggie of Raphael in the Vatican, in forty three prints.

The Farnesina Fresoes.

21. Venus pointing out Psyche to Cupid.
22. Cupid showing Psyche to the Graces.
23. Venus parting from Juno and Ceres in anger, Venus in her chariot.
24. Venus praying Jove to send Mercury for Psyche.
25. Mercury proclaiming the orders of Jove concerning Psyche.
26. Psyche borne by three Amorini, carrying the vase of beauty which she has received from Proserpine, to appease the anger of Venus.
27. Psyche presenting the vase of beauty to Venus, Jove saluting Cupid.
28. Mercury conducting Psyche to Heaven.
29. Venus and Cupid pleading before the Council of the Gods.
30. The Mariage feast of Cupid and Psyche.
31. The Triumph of Galatea.

The following are also by Raphael Sanzio.

32. The Transfiguration.	Vatican.	Rome
33. The Madonna di Fuligno.	"	"
34. The Coronation of the Virgin.	"	"
35. The Entombment, in the Borghese Gallery.		"
36. The Sibyls in the Church of St. Maria della Pace.		
37. The Mariage of the Virgin.		Milan.
38. The Madonna di San Sisto.		Dresden.
39. The Madonna della Seggiola.		Florence.
40. La Bella Giardiniera.		Paris.
41. The Madonna del Pesce.		Madrid.
42. Holy Family.		Naples.
43. The Madonna dei Fiori.		Paris
44. St. John in the Wilderness.		Florence.
45. St. Cecilia.		Bologna.
46. The Madonna del Cardellino.		Florence.
47. Lo Spasimo di Sicilia.		Madrid.
48. The Madonna; Colonna Gallery.		Rome.

The Sistine Chapel Series

49. The prophet Isaiah.
50.   "   Jeremiah.
51.   "   Ezechiel.
52.   "   Daniel.
53.   "   Zachariah.
54.   "   Joel.
55.   "   Jonah.
56. The Sibyl Persica.
57.   "   Erythraea.
58.   "   Delphica.
59. The Sibyl Libica
60.   "   Cumaea.
61. Moses showing the brazen Serpent to the people.
62. David slaying Goliath.
63. The execution of Haman.
64. Judith with the head of Holofernes.

65. Moses meeting with the daughter of Raguel at the well	Botticelli
66. The circumcision of the children of Moses.	Perugino
67. The overthrow of Pharoah and his host in the Red Sea.	Rosselli
68. The Israelites worshipping the Golden Calf.	
69. The destruction of Korah, Dathan, and Abiram.	Botticelli
70. The last address of Moses, and appointment of Joshua.	Luca Signorelli
71. The Baptism of our Lord.	Perugino.
72. The Temptation in the Wilderness.	Botticelli.
73. The Calling of Peter and Andrew.	Ghirlandaio
74. The Sermon on the Mount.	Rosselli.
75. The Last Supper.	"
76. Our Lord giving the keys to St. Peter.	Perugino.

Miscellaneous.

77. The Last Supper.	Leonardo da Vinci,		Milan.
78. The Deposition from the Cross.	Daniele di Volterra,		Rome.
79. The Madonna enthroned with Saints.	Perugino,	Vatican.	"
80. The Communion of St. Jerome.	Domenichino,	"	"
81. The Cumean Sibyl.	"	Borghese,	"
82. The chase of Diana.	"		"
83. The Martyrdom of St. Sebastian.	"	St. Maria degli Angeli,	"
84. The Martyrdom of St. Andrew.	"	St. Gregorio,	"
85. St. John.			St. Petersburg.
86. The Magdalen.	Correggio.		Dresden.
87. Madonna della Scodella.	"		Parma.
88. Madonna col divoto.	"		Munich.
89. Madonna and St. Jerome.	"		Parma.
90. Madonna del Cardellino.	Guercino.		
91. Ecce Homo.	"		
92. The Sibyl Persica.	"	Capitol,	Rome.
93. The Aurora.	"	Villa Lodovisi,	"
94. The daughters of Lot.	"		
95. The Immaculate Conception.	Murillo.		Paris.
96. The Magdalen.	"		London.
97. The Madonna del Sacco.	Andrea del Sarto.		Florence.
98. The Deposition from the Cross.	"		
99. The Madonna of Lucca.	Fra Bartolomeo.		Lucca.
100. The Assumption of the Virgin.	Titian.		
101. La Bella Donna.	"		
102. Wife of Titian.	"		
103. Beatrice Cenci.	Guido Reni.	Barberini,	Rome.
104. The Aurora.	"	Rospigliosi,	"
105. The Crucifixion.	"	Church of S. Lorenzo in Lucina.	"
106. The Annunciation.	"	Quirinal, Palace.	"
107. St. Michael.	"	Cappuccini,	"
108. The deposition from the Cross.	Rubens.		Antwerp.
109. The Madonna with cradle.	"		London.
110. The Madonna.	Carlo Dolci.	Corsini	Rome
111. The Christ.	"		
112. Mount Parnassus.	Raphael Mengs.	Villa Albani.	"
113. The Family of Charles I. of England.	Vandyke		
114. The Cavallo Bianco (Francis di Moncada).	"		
115. The death of St. Francis.	Benouville.		
116. Venus and Cupid.	Pompeo Battoni.		
117. Venus in the shell.	Bernardino Nocchi.		
118. Leda and the swan.	Correggio.		
119. The Hours.	Poussin.		
120. Cupids rejoicing at the carrying away of Proserpine.	Albani.		
121. St. Cecilia.	G. Gandolfi.		
122. Madonna.	Sassoferrato		
123. Madonna.	"		
124. Madonna with Infant sleeping.	"		
125. " " " standing.			
126. A Friar preaching, in the Coliseum.	M. G. Brennan		
127. Judith showing the head of Holofernes to the people.	Benvenuto		
128. Tomb of Clement the XIII. in St. Peter's by Canova			
129. St. John, by Domenichino.			
130. Marriage of the Virgin, by Guercino.			
131. Susannah and the Elders, by Giovanni della Valle.			
132. The Goddesses preparing for the judgment of Paris, by Piero ...			
133. Perseus slaying Medusa, by Annibale Carracci.			
134. The family of the Gracchi, by Camuccini.			
135. Awaking, from a picture by Greuze.			

Catalogue of Macpherson's photographs of prints and engravings. (Coll. P. Becchetti, Rome).

44

MACPHERSON'S
VATICAN SCULPTURES,

134 in all, including six Interiors of the Vatican.

1ST MARCH, 1868

Braccio nuovo

1. Caryatide.
2. Dacian Captive.
3. Silenus nursing Bacchus.
4. Augustus, statue found recently at Prima Porta.
5. Æsculapius.
6. Pudicitia, or Livia.
7. Faun.
8. Caryatide.
9. Diana contemplating Endymion.
10. Euripides.
11. Julia, daughter of Titus.
12. Plenty.
13. Demosthenes.
14. Apoxyomenos.
15. Wounded Amazon.
16. Fortune.
17. Ceres.
18. Venus Anadyomene.
19. The River Nile.
20. Tauric (Crimean) Diana, sometimes called the Juno Regina.
21. Minerva Medica.
22. Dacian Captive.
23. Faun of Praxiteles.
24. Lucius Verus.

Chiaramonte.

25. Fragment of a draped female statue.
26. Juno nursing Mars, or Hercules.
27. The Theban Hercules.
28. Venus from the bath.
29. Latona in Delos.
30. Venus from the bath.
31. Tiberius Seated, wearing the Civic-Crown.
32. Bust of the Young Augustus.
33. Draped female statue.
34. Diadumenianus.
35. Portrait-statue of Tiberius seated.
36. Cupid of Praxiteles.
37. Bust of Cato.
38. Bust of Ariadne.
39. Bust, called a Meleager.
40. Silenus.
41. Cuirass and head of Drusus.
42. Group of Bacchus and Faun, removed from the Sala Rotonda.
43. Hercules and Telephus.
44. Hygeia, fragment of a group.
45. Hercules in repose.

Egyptian Museum

46. The Egyptian Antinous.

Pio Clementino.

47. The Torso Belvedere.
48. Fragment of a draped male figure with Greek sandals.
49. Fragment of a draped male torso.
50. Fragment of a seated female figure draped.
51. The Meleager.
52. A Sarcophagus, Bacchic Dance.
53. Venus and Cupid.
54. The Mercury of the Belvedere.
55. Fragment of a draped female figure on a Dolphin.
56. The Laocöon.
57. Hygeia or Isis Salutaria.
58. Apollo Belvedere.

Hall of the Animals.

59. A Mithraic Group.
60. Triton bearing off a Nymph.

Hall of Statues.

61. Clodius Albinus.
62. Cupid. (a fragment called the Genius of the Vatican).
63. Penelope.
64. Caius Caligula.
65. Apollo Saurocthonos.
66. Amazon stringing her bow.
67. The Drunken Faun.
68. Posidippus.
69. Bust of Menelaus.
70. Bust of Nero Citharedo.
71. Menander.
72. A Danaide.
73. Ariadne in Naxos.
74. Bas-relief of Theseus abandoning Ariadne.
75. Lucius Verus, portrait-statue in armour.
76. A Dancer.
77. The Crouching Venus.
78. Diana Lucifera.
79. Faun in Rosso Antico. } Smaller Cabinet.

Hall of the Muses.

80. Silenus.
81. Bacchus in female attire.
82. Melpomene, the Tragic Muse.
83. Thalia, the Comic Muse.
84. Urania, the Muse of Astronomy.
85. Clio, the Historic Muse.
86. Polyhymnia, the Mimic Muse, also of the Sacred Hymn.
87. Erato, the Lyric Muse.
88. Calliope, the Epic Muse.
89. Apollo Musagete, or Citharedo.
90. Bust or Herma of Themistocles.
91. Terpischore, Muse of the Sacred Dance.
92. Euterpe, the Muse of Music.
93. Aspasia veiled.
94. Sappho.
95. Pericles.

Hall called the Rotonda.

96. Tragedy.
97. Comedy.
98. Bust of the Jupiter of Otricoli.
99. The Antinous, late of the Lateran.
100. Bust of Faustina.
101. The veiled Augustus.
102. Bust of Hadrian.
103. Gilt bronze Hercules, found in the recent excavations of Pompey's theatre.
104. Bust of Antinous.
105. Antoninus Pius.
106. Bust of Oceanus.
107. Nerva Coccius.
108. Bust of Jupiter Serapis.
109. Ceres, (known as the Barberini Juno.)
110. Bust of Claudius.
111. Juno Sospita.
112. Plotina, bust.
113. Domna Julia, bust.
114. Juno, called a Ceres.
115. Bust of Publius Elvius Pertinax.

Hall of the Greek Cross

116. Venus of Cnidos.
117. The Indian Bacchus.

Hall of the Biga.

118. Young Athlete.
119. Portrait Statue, called Phocian.
120. The Discobolus of Myron.
121. The Huntress Diana.
122. The Biga.

Hall of the Candelabra

123. Diana of Ephesus.
124. The Ancient Fisherman.
125. Boy and Swan.
126. Virgin Racer, of the Olympian Games.
127. Antinous with the attributes of Vertumnus, formerly in the Braccio nuovo. (see N. 4 of small volume.)
128. Venus Gabina, formerly in the Chiaramonte Museum, now removed. (see N. 42 of small volume.)

N. B. -- Visitors travelling with Murray's Hand book" are informed that a correspondence with Mr. Murray, on the subject of misrepresentations contained in the Handbook for Rome, has been printed : copies of which may be had on application to Mr Macpherson

Catalogue of Macpherson's photographs of the Vatican Sculptures, 1 March 1868. (Coll. P. Becchetti, Rome).

MACPHERSON'S
SCULPTURES OF THE CAPITOL
287 in all.

The complete Volume, 300 francs. They may be had separately at one franc and a half each.

This Volume is intended as a companion to that of the Vatican Sculptures containing 134, the price of which is 150 francs or separately at one franc and a half each.

ROME December 1871

Hall of the Conservatori.

1. The bronze Wolf of the Capitol.
2. The thorn-picker.
3. Apotheosis of Faustina the younger.
4. Marcus Aurelius reading a memorial.
5. Marcus Aurelius offering a sacrifice.
6. Marcus Aurelius in a Quadriga.
7. Marcus Aurelius receiving the submission of the Parthians.
8. Marcus Aurelius receiving the Globe from the hands of Rome.
9. Colossal statue of Julius Caesar.

Basreliefs from the Arch of Marcus Aurelius, destroyed in the Pontificate of Alexander VII.

Square of the Capitol.

10. Colossal equestrian statue of Marcus Aurelius.
11. Recumbent statue of the River Nile.
12. Statue of Rome triumphant.
13. Recumbent Statue of the Tiber.

Cortile of the Museum of Sculpture.

14. Recumbent statue, styled « Marforio ».
15. A Satyr.
16. A Satyr.
17. A sarcophagus with bas-relief of the chase of boar and deer.
18. A sarcophagus, with marine monsters.

Ground Floor.

19. Endymion.
20. A sarcophagus, with Bacchus and Bacchante.
21. A sarcophagus, bearing a greek inscription.
22. A sarcophagus, with bas-relief of the chase of the Calydonian Boar.
23. A sarcophagus, with bas-relief of the chase of Boar and Stag.
24. Monument found at Porta Salara in 1871.
25. Colossal Statue of Diana.
26. A sarcophagus, with the Calydonian chase.
27. A sarcophagus, transferred from the steps of the Ara-Coeli.
28. A sarcophagus, representing a battle between Romans and Gauls.
29. A sarcophagus, with the Story of Achilles and Briseis.

Gallery.

30. Bust of Marcus Aurelius.
31. Bust of Faustina.
32. Bust of Septimius Severus.
33. Bust — (incognito).
34. Seated Statue of Silenus.
35. A Lion, life-size, in marble.
36. An ideal female figure, half-length.
37. Statue of a piping Faun.
38. Cupid bending his bow, by Praxiteles.
39. Bust of Silenus.
40. A sarcophagus, with the story of Prometheus.
41. Bust — (incognito).
42. Bust — (incognito).
43. A sarcophagus, with the story of Diana and Endymion.
44.
45. Male Busts. — (incogniti).
46.
47. Male Busts. — (incogniti).
48.
49. Male Busts. — (incogniti).
50. Bust of a youth with helmet — (incognito).
51.
52. Male Busts. — (incognito).
53. A statue of Innocence.
54. A mosaic, representing the Doves of Sosus.
55. Statue of the Emperor Decius.
56. Bust. — (incognito).
57. Statue of Agrippina with the infant Nero.
58. Statue of an old Bacchante intoxicated.
59. Female bust. — (incognito).
60. Sarcophagus, with bas-relief of the rape of Proserpine.
61. Statue, semi-nude. — (incognito).
62. Bust of a laughing Faun.
63. Hercules strangling the serpents.
64. A head of Paris.
65. Bust. — (incognito).
66. Bust of Lucilla, daughter of Marcus Aurelius.
67. Statue of the Muse Euterpe.
68. Statue of a Faun playing on a flute.
69. A colossal head of Niobe.
70. Fighting Gladiator.
71. Colossal head of Juno.
72. Colossal head of Venus.
73. One of the sons of Niobe.
74. One of the daughters of Niobe.
75. Bust of Jupiter; styled « Della Valle ».
76. Statue of Diana Lucifera.
77. A sarcophagus, with the story of Bacchus.
78. Bust. — (incognito).
79. Seated statue of a personage with the rank of Consul.
80. Statue of Psyche.
81. Cupid and Psyche.
82. The Venus of the Capitol.
83. Statue of Leda.
84. Seated statue of Julia Moesa.
85. Bust of Jupiter Ammon.
86. Seated statue of Ceres.
87. Statue of a Muse, with the Genius of Music.
88. Bust of Tiberius.
89. Statue of Jupiter.

Catalogue of Macpherson's photographs of the Capitoline Sculptures, December 1871. (Coll. P. Becchetti, Rome).

90. Statue of Bacchus.
91. Bust of Augustus.
92. Bust of Jupiter Serapis.
93. Bust of Julia Sabina.
94. Bust of the young Marcus Aurelius.
95. Statue of Minerva Pacifera.
96. Bust of Trajan.
97. Bust of Silenus crowned with ivy.
98. Bust. — (incognito).
99. A colossal Vase, found on the Appian Way, near the tomb of Cecilia Metella.

Hall of the Emperors.

100. Bust of Julius Caesar.
101. Bust of Augustus.
102. Bust of Marcellus.
103. Bust of Tiberius.
104. Bust of Drusus the elder.
105. Bust of Drusus the younger.
106. Bust of Antonia the younger, wife of the elder Drusus.
107. Bust of Germanicus.
108. Bust of Caligula, in basalt.
109. Bust of Claudius.
110. Bust of Messalina.
111. Bust of Agrippina the younger, the mother of Nero.
112. Bust of Nero.
113. Bust of Poppea, the second wife of Nero.
114. Bust of Galba.
115. Bust of Otho.
116. Bust of Vitellius.
117. Bust of Vespasian.
118. Bust of Titus Vespasian.
119. Bust of Julia, daughter of Titus.
120. Bust of Domitian.
121. Bust of Domitia Longina, wife of Domitian.
122. Bust of Nerva.
123. Bust of Marciana, sister of Trajan.
124. Bust of Matidia, niece of Trajan.
125. Bust of Hadrian.
126. Bust of Julia Sabina, wife of Hadrian.
127. Bust of Lucius Verus, adopted by Antoninus Pius.
128. Bust of Antoninus Pius.
129. Bust of Faustina the elder, wife of Antoninus Pius.
130. Bust of the youthful Marcus Aurelius.
131. Bust of Marcus Aurelius.
132. Bust of Faustina the younger, wife of Marcus Aurelius.
133. Bust of Galerius Antoninus, son of Antoninus Pius.
134. Bust of Lucius Verus.
135. Bust of Lucilla, wife of Lucius Verus.
136. Bust of Commodus.
137. Bust of Crispina, wife of Commodus.
138. Bust of Pertinax.
139. Bust of Didius Julianus.
140. Bust of Manlia Scantilla, wife of Didius Julianus.
141. Bust of Pescennius Niger.
142. Bust of Clodius Albinus.
143. Bust of Septimius Severus.
144. Bust of Septimius Severus, in alabaster.
145. Bust of Julia Pia, wife of Septimius Severus.
146. Bust of Caracalla.
147. Bust of Geta, the brother of Caracalla.
148. Bust of Macrinus.

149. Bust of Diadumenianus.
150. Bust of Heliogabalus.
151. Bust of Annia Faustina, third wife of Heliogabalus.
152. Bust of Julia Moesa.
153.
154. Busts of Alexander Severus, and his mother Julia Mamaea.
155. Bust of Julius Maximinus.
156. Bust of Maximus.
157. Bust of the elder Gordianus.
158. Bust of Gordianus the younger.
159. Bust of Maximus Pupienus.
160. Bust of Caelius Balbinus.
161. Bust of Gordianus Pius, son of Gordianus the younger.
162. Bust of Julius Philippus the younger.
163. Bust of Decius.
164. Bust of Quintus Erennius, eldest son of Decius.
165. Bust of Hostilianus, younger son of Decius.
166. Bust of Trebonianus Gallus.
167. Bust of Volusianus, son of Trebonianus Gallus.
168. Bust of Gallienus, son of Valerian.
169. Bust of Carinus, son of Carus.
170. Bust of Diocletian.
171. Bust of Constantius Chlorus, father of Constantine.
172. Bust of Julian the Apostate.
173. Bust of Decentius Magnus.
174. A seated statue of Agrippina the mother of Nero.

Hall of Illustrious Men.

175. Seated statue of Marcus Marcellus, conqueror of Syracuse.
176. Bust of Virgil.
177. Bust of Heraclitus.
178. Bust of Socrates.
179. Bust of Alcibiades.
180. Bust of Aristides.
181. Bust of Seneca.
182. Bust of Marcus Agrippa.
183. Bust of Diogenes.
184. Bust of Archimedes.
185. Bust of Thales.
186. Bust of Pythagoras.
187. Bust of Aristophanes.
188. Bust of Demosthenes.
189. Bust of Sophocles.
190. Bust of Persius Flaccus.
191. Bust of Anacreon.
192. Bust of Hippocrates.
193. Bust of Aratus.
194. Bust of Democritus.
195. Bust of Euripides.
196. Bust of Homer.
197. Veiled bust of Homer.
198. Bust of Corbulo.
199. Bust of Scipio Africanus.
200. Bust of Aristomachus.
201. Bust of Pompey the Great.
202. Bust of Cato.
203. Bust of Aristotle.
204. Bust of Cleopatra.
205. Bust of Herodotus.
206. Bust of Cecrops.

(Contd.) *Catalogue of Macpherson's photographs of the Capitoline Sculptures, December 1871.*

207. Bust of Thucydides.
208. Bust of Aeschines.
209. Bust of Epicurus.
210. Twin-bust of Epicurus and Metrodorus.
211. Bust of Epicurus.
212. Bust of Phocion.
213. Bust of Masinissa, the Numidian.
214. Bust of Antisthenes.
215. Bust of Domitian Enobarbus.
216. Bust of Cicero.
217. Bust of Terentius.
218. Bust of Apollonius of Tyana.
219. Bust of Archytas of Tarentum.
220. Bust of Eschylus.

Saloon.

221. Statue of Jupiter, in nero antico.
222. A Centaur.
223. Statue of a youthful Hercules.
224. A Centaur.
225. Statue of Esculapius, in nero-antico.
226. Statue of Hygeia.
227. Statue of Apollo, in the Archaic style.
228. Statue of a youthful Apollo, touching the lyre.
229. Statue of Marcus Aurelius, in armour.
230. Statue of a wounded Amazon.
231. Roman portrait statues, under the semblance of Mars and Venus.
232. Statue of a Muse, holding lotos-blossoms.
233. Statue of Minerva, with the Aegis.
234. Statue of a Faun.
235. Statue of the Apollo of Pyxus.
236. Statue of Minerva, armed.
237. Colossal bust of Trajan, wearing the civic crown.
238. Statue of Augustus.
239. Statue of the Empress Lucilla, under the semblance of Ceres.
240. Statue of an Athlete.
241. Statue of Hadrian.
242. Statue of Caius Marius as Consul.
243. Statue of Julia Pia as Vesta.
244. Gilt-bronze statue of Hercules.
345. Statue of a wounded Amazon.
246. Statue of Ptolemy.
247. Statue of a gymnast, (Pancratiast).
248. Statue of a Praefica (a hired mourner); also supposed to represent Hecuba, or the nurse of the children of Niobe.
249. Statue of Thalia.

250. Statue of Clemency.
251. Colossal bust of Antoninus Pius.
252. Statue of Diana.
253. Statue of the hunter Politimus (with name on base).
254. Statue of Harpocrates.

Hall of the red marble Faun.

255. Statue of a Faun, in rosso-antico
256. Colossal bust of Hercules.
257. Small statue of Diana.
258. Bust of the Consul Cethegus, with inscription, Cethego. VC. L. Macchius Graccus.
259. Sarcophagus, with the story of Diana and Endymion.
260. Head of a Satyr.
261. Statue of a boy, playing with a mask.
262. Statue of Pallas.
263. Bust of Marcus Aurelius, at an advanced age.
264. Small statue of Alexander the Great, in armour.
265. Bust of Marcus Brutus.
266. Statue of Isis.
267. Male bust. — (incognito).
268. Group of a boy and swan.
269. Colossal mask of a Satyr.
270. Bust of Ariadne. (eyeless).
271. A sepulchral Urn, with the battle between Theseus and the Amazons.
272. Male bust — (incognito), on which is inscribed « Latu ».

Hall of the Dying Gladiator.

273. The Dying Gladiator. — (front view).
274. The Dying Gladiator. — (back view).
275. Statue of the Lycian Apollo.
276. Statue of Plenty.
277. Bust of Ariande.
278. Heroic statue of an Amazon.
279. Bust of Alexander the Great.
280. Statue of Juno.
281. Bust of Marcus Brutus.
282. Statue of Isis.
283. Statue of Flora.
284. Statue of Antinous.
285. The Faun of Praxiteles.
286. Statue of Pandora.
287. Statue of Zeno.

(Contd.) *Catalogue of Macpherson's photographs of the Capitoline Sculptures, December 1871.*

MACPHERSON'S

PHOTOGRAPHS,

12 Vicolo d'Alibert.

ROME

DECEMBER 1871

THE PHOTOGRAPHS NAMED IN THIS LIST ARE OF ONE UNIFORM PRICE, NAMELY 3 FRANCS EACH

* 1. Arch of Constantine — South façade.
* 2. Arch of Constantine — North façade.
* 3. Arch of Constantine — North façade, including the Meta Sudans. and a portion of the Convent of St. Bonaventura.
4. The Fountain of Trevi.
5.
6. A view of the Temple of Pallas taking in the figure of Minerva in the centre.
7. Columns of the Forum of Nerva, and the Arch called « L'Arco de'Pantani. »
8. The three Columns at the foot of the Capitol, formerly styled the Temple of Jupiter Tonans, and the Arch of Septimius Severus.
9. The eight Columns at the foot of the Capitol, formerly styled the Temple of Concord, and now the Temple of Vespasian or Temple of Saturn.
10. A view of the same in extreme profile, including a portion of the Basilica of Constantine, Phoca's Column, and the Arch of Titus.
11.
* 12. Temple of Venus and Rome with distant view of the Roman Forum; taken from the Coliseum.
* 13. Excavations of the Julian Basilica, including a view of the various Temples in the Forum, with the Arch of Titus in the distance.
14. Base of the Column in the Forum of Trajan.
* 15.
* 16. Forum Romanum — General view taken from the Clivus Capitolinus, and including the principal Temples in the Forum, and the Arch of Titus.
* 17. Temple of Vesta, Temple of Fortuna Virilis, and the House of Rienzi.
* 18.
* 19. Temple of Vesta and the Fountain, taken in summer.
20. Forum of Trajan.
21. Side view of the Temple dedicated to Antoninus and Faustina, Roman Forum.
* 22. View of the « Ponte Rotto » with the new Suspension bridge.
23. Façade of the Church of St. John Lateran.
* 24. Ruin called the Temple of Minerva Medica.
* 25. The garden-front of the Villa Medici, built from the design of Michael-Angelo — on the Pincian Hill.
* 26. The Porta Maggiore.
27. Arch of Titus, Roman Forum.
28. Bas-relief in the interior of the Arch of Titus, representing the procession of the seven-branched Candlestick.
29. Equestrian bronze Statue of Marcus Aurelius, standing in the square of the Capitol.
* 30. The Coliseum with Meta Sudans and portion of the Via Sacra.
* 31. The Coliseum with the Arch of Constantine.
* 32.
33. Portion of the interior wall of the Coliseum.
* 34. The Castle and bridge of St. Angelo, with the Vatican in the distance.
* 35. The Castle St. Angelo, on a larger scale.
* 36. The Garden in the Vatican styled « della Pigna » containing the marble base of a Column dedicated to Antoninus; architecture of Bramante.
* 37. Bas-relief on the base of the Antonine Column, representing the Apotheosis of Antoninus and Faustina; in the Garden of the Vatican.
* 38 - 39. Bas-reliefs representing funeral games, on the other sides of the base of the Antonine Column.
* 40. Fountain of the piazza Barberini.

* 41. Basilica of Constantine, formerly called the Temple of Peace, the Forum.
42.
* 43. Church of Santa Maria Maggiore.
* 44.
* 45. Tomb of Cecilia Metella, with distant view of Rome.
* 46.
* 47. Temple of Fortuna Virilis, and the house of Rienzi.
48. Cloisters of St. Paul's Basilica, out-side the walls of Rome
49. Arch of Titus, from the temple of Venus and Rome.
50. Base of the Obelisk and Fountain in the Piazza Navona.
51. Church of the Trinità de'Monti.
52. Front of a Gothic Church at Vicovaro, near Tivoli.
53. Church of Santa Maria in Cosmedin; called the « Bocca della Verità ».
54. Arch of the Consul Dolabella on the Celian Hill.
* 55. View of the Capitoline Hill, from the foot of the Aventine.
56.
* 57. Piazza of St. Peter's.
58.
* 59.
* 61. Piazza of St. Peter's, on a smaller scale than n. 57.
* 60. Piazza of St. Peter's, and the Vatican.
* 62.
63. Group of Stone pines in the Villa Doria.
64. Cypresses planted by Michael-Angelo, in the Cloisters of Santa Maria degli Angeli.
65.
66. Arch of Septimius Severus, in the Roman Forum.
* 67. View of the Cloaca Maxima, Temple of Vesta, Church of the « Bocca della Verità » etc.
* 68. The three Columns, formerly called the Temple of Jupiter Stator, and now styled Minerva Chalcidica, with the Temples of Peace, Antoninus and Faustina, etc. in the Roman Forum.
* 69.
70. House of Lucrezia Borgia near the Church of San Pietro in Vincula.
* 71. A painting by Enghert representing an episode in Sicilian history viz: the arrest of the family of Manfred by order of Charles d'Anjou.
* 72.
73. Bas-relief by Gibson, Phaeton guiding the Chariot and horses of the Sun.
74.
75. The Apollo Belvedere.
76. Arch of the Goldsmiths, sometimes called the little Arch of Septimius Severus, in the Forum Boarium.
77. Profile view of the Statue of Livia, also called the Pudicitia, in the Braccio nuovo, Vatican Museum.
78. The Sleeping Ariadne, formerly called the Cleopatra; Hall of the Philosophers; Vatican.
* 79.
80. The Bull-Slayer, Hall of the Animals; Vatican.
81. The Laocoon; Vatican Museum.
* 82. The Nile and its tributaries; Vatican.
* 83. The Roman Campagna, near the Frascati Railway.
* 84. View of Tombs on the Via Appia.
* 85.
86.
87.
88.
89.
90. Front view of the Livia of the Vatican, commonly called the Pudicitia.
91.
92.
93. Ulysses, statue by Macdonald.
94. The Piazza del Popolo, looking from the Corso.
* 95. Sibyls of Raphael; in the church of S. Maria della Pace
* 96. The Quirinal Hill with the obelisk and Horses.
97. The Statue of Moses, by Michael-Angelo, in the Church of San Pietro in Vincula.
* 98.
99. - Sabina - statue by Cardwell.
* 100.
* 101. View on the Campagna 4 miles from the Lateran gate, on the Naples road.

Catalogue of views by Macpherson, December 1871. (Coll. P. Becchetti, Rome).

* 102. View of the Acqueduct. — Acqua-Claudia
* 103. Large view of the Claudian Acqueduct.
* 104. Easter Benediction at St. Peter's.
105.
106. Statue of the Indian, by Crawford.
* 107.
* 108. Porta Furba, Frascati road.
109. The Discobulus throwing the discus; Vatican.
* 110. Palace of the Cesars on the Palatine.
* 111. Arch of Septimius Severus looking from the Forum.
* 112. Arch of Janus Quadrifrons.
113.
114. Temple of the Sibyl, front view.
115. — on a larger scale.
116. — seen from the bridge.
117. — — from the opposite side of the Ravine.
118. Large Waterfall. Tivoli.
119. Cascatelle at the Villa of Mecenas. Tivoli.
* 120. Temple styled « Della Tosse » Tivoli.
121. Cypresses in the Villa d'Este. Tivoli.
122. The Ravine, with Temple of the Sybil and Grotto of Neptune. Tivoli.
* 123. Castle of Tivoli.
* 124.
* 125. Ponte Lugano — with the Tomb of Plautius.
* 126. The Valley of the Anio, with the upper and lower Cascatelle, Mecenas's Villa and distant Campagna.
* 127. Palazzo Altoviti on the Tiber.
* 128. Pyramid of Caius Cestius, and the English burying ground.
129. Madonna and Child, from the original painting by Sasso-Ferrato.
130.
131.
* 132. Side-door on the left with bas-reliefs. Cathedral of Orvieto.
* 133. Bas-reliefs illustrative of the history of Christ.
* 134. Bas-relief of the Last Judgment, « Paradise and Hell ».
* 135. Etruscan gateway, Perugia.
* 136. Fountain in the Piazza del Duomo, at Perugia.
137. Church of San Bernardino, Perugia.
138. Temple of Clitumnus.
139. Falls of Terni.
140.
141. Royal Palace at Caprarola.
142. Façade of the Church of Santa Maria at Toscanella.
143. Principal doorway of the above.
* 144. Group from a fresco by Luca Signorelli at Orvieto.
145. - Amor Victor, - a group by Cartwell.
* 146. Piazza del Popolo, looking south.
147.
* 148. Horses of the Capitol from the Palazzo Caffarelli.
* 149. View over Rome from the Palatine Hill.
150. Bas-relief of the Biga — Arch of Titus.
151. Window in the House of Lucrezia Borgia.
* 152. Piazza and Fontain of the Tartarughe.
153. Tomb of Cecilia Metella from the road, - Via Appia -.
* 154. The Cloaca Maxima.
155.
* 156.
157. Grotto of Egeria.
158. Porta San Lorenzo.
159. Statue of Minerva Medica.
160. Statue of Demosthenes.
161. Statue of Silenus holding Bacchus.
162.
163. The Theatre of Marcellus, from the Piazza Montanara.
* 164. Phoca's Column, and temples in the Forum, including the recent restoration of the remains of the school of Xanthus.
165. Broken Arches in the Coliseum.
* 166 Julian Basilica looking towards the Tabularium.
* 167. Porta San Paolo from within, and the Pyramid of Caius Cestius.
* 168. The temple of Antoninus and Faustina similar to n. 21, but on a larger scale.
* 169. Distant view of Rome and the baths of Caracalla, from St. John of the Latin Gate.
* 170. Ruins of the Baronial Stronghold at Nepi, hunting seat of Lucrezia Borgia.

* 171. Valley of the Tiber at Ponte Felice near Borghettaccio, between Civita Castellana and Otricoli.
172. The bridge of Augustus at Narni, from the modern bridge.
* 173. The bridge of Augustus at Narni, looking towards the modern bridge.
174. Temple of Clitumnus. smaller than n. 138.
175..
* 176. General view of Assisi, from Santa Maria degli Angeli..
177. The Church of San Ruffino, Cathedral of Assisi.
178 The Temple of Minerva in the Forum of Assisi.
179. Church of San Francesco at Assisi, from the Via Superba.
* 180. Church of San Francesco at Assisi, from the lower piazza near the gate.
181 The doorway and portico of the Middle Church or Crypt of San Francesco, at Assisi.
* 182. Fortress at Perugia built by Pope Paul III, shewing an ancient Etruscan gateway.
* 183. The Corso of Perugia with the Palazzo Comunale.
* 184. The Fountain of the Pisani at Perugia, looking towards the Duomo.
* 185.
* 186.
* 187.
* 188. Tomb of Scipio. Vatican.
* 189. Villa Mellini. Monte Mario.
190. Fresco of P. Perugino at Panicale.
* 191. Greek theatre at Tusculum.
192- Tivoli, from the Olive-grove below the cascatelle.
193. Donkey-road in the Olive-grove. below Tivoli.
* 194.
195. Grotto of the Sibyl, at Tivoli.
* 196. Convent of « San Cosimato » near Vicovaro, above Tivoli.
* 197. The bridge and Franciscan convent at Subiaco.
* 198. Subiaco, from the Franciscan convent.
* 199. Benedictine convent called the « Sacro Specco » at Subiaco.
* 200. Subiaco, from the chapel of the Madonna near Sta. Scolastica.
201. Portion of the garden-façade and staircase of the Lancellotti palace at Velletri.
202. The porticoed Belvedere of the Lancellotti palace, Velletri.
203. The Belvedere of the Lancellotti palace at Velletri, looking towards the open end.
204. Doric temple, said to have been erected to Hercules, at Cora.
205. Remains of the temple of Castor and Pollux, at Cora.
* 206. The deserted city of Ninfa, in the Pontine Marshes.
207.
2008. General view of the city and fortress of Sermoneta.
* 209. Sermoneta, with Norma, Ninfa, and the Volscian maremma.
* 210. The Abbey-church at Fossa-nuova near Sonino.
211 Cloisters in the Abbey at Fossa-nuova.
212 One of the Vatican fountains in the Piazza of St. Peter's.
* 213.
* 214. The Cliff of Terracina, with the remains of an Imperial Villa and the temple of Jupiter Anxurus.
* 215. The road on the beach approaching Terracina from Fondi.
* 216. The Pontine Marshes at Badino, Monte Circeo in the distance.
217.
* 218.
* 219.
* 220.
* 221.
* 222.
* 223.
* 224
225.
* 226. The Ponte Nomentana over the Anio.
* 227. The Ponte Nomentana, and general view from the Mons Sacer.
* 228. The tomb of Virginia at the Mons Sacer, taking in the Ponte Nomentana
* 229.
* 230.
* 231.
* 232.
* 233. View over Rome, taking in the Vatican, from Monte Pincio.
* 234. The Palatine Hill, from the Tabularium.
* 235. The Arch of Septimius Severus, from the Tabularium.
* 236. The Cloaca Maxima, shewing the inner arch.
* 237. The Pantheon, from the Piazza della Rotonda.

(Contd.) *Catalogue of views by Macpherson, December 1871.*

238. The temple of Mars Ultor, in the Forum of Nerva.
239. Interior of the gallery called the Braccio-nuovo, in the Vatican.
240. Interior of the Chiaramonte Museum in the Vatican.
241. The Hall of the Animals, in the Vatican.
242. The gallery of the ... , sometimes called the Hall of the Philosophers, Vatican.
243. Hall of the Greek Cross, Vatican.
244. Hall of the Candelabra, Vatican.
245. The "Apoxyomenos" statue of an athlete, Vatican.
246. The Egyptian Antinous in the Vatican.
247. Statue of Meleager in the Vatican.
248. Statue of Mercury, sometimes called the Antinous of the Belvedere, Vatican.
* 249. The Biga of the Vatican.
250. The Antinous, late of the Lateran Museum.
251. The dancing Silenus, in the Lateran Museum.
252. A monument and sarcophagus, in the Christian Museum of the Lateran.
253. Sitting statue of Bishop Hypolitus in the Christian Museum of the Lateran.
254. Tomb of Julius II, in the church of San Pietro in Vincula.
* 255. The Roman Forum, from the Tabularium.
256. The Discobulus of the Palazzo Massimo.
* 257. The bridge and castle of St. Angelo (similar to n. 34 but not oval).
258. Statue of Sophocles, in the Lateran Museum.
* 259.
* 260.
261. One of the Loggie of Raphael; Vatican.
262. Interior of the Vatican Library.
* 263. Casino built by Pius IV in the gardens of the Vatican, architecture of Pirro Ligorio.
264. The Torso Belvedere, Vatican.
* 265. The Massacre of the Innocents, from an engraving by Marc-Antonio.
266.
267.
268.
269. Madonna and Child with Saints, from the original picture by Lo Spagna, in the town hall at Spoleto.
270. Façade of the Cathedral (Sta. Maria), at Spoleto.
* 271. Large details of the portico of the Cathedral at Spoleto. Architecture of Bramante.
* 272. The repulse of Hannibal at Spoleto, from a picture by Francesco Coghetti of Bergamo.
* 273.
274. The Church of St. John of the Latin gate; Rome.
275.
276. Madonna and Child by Leonardo da Vinci at Sant' Onofrio, from a drawing by Agricola.
277. Madonna and Child from the original cartoon by Giulio Romano, now in Prussia.
278. Iris, from the original picture by Guido Head in St. Luke's Academy.
* 279. Fragment of the frieze of the Basilica of Trajan, preserved in the Lateran Museum.
280.
* 281. The great staircase in the Castle of Bracciano.
* 282. Socrates, statue in the Campana Museum, now in France.
* 283. Faustina, statue in the Campana Museum, now in Russia.
* 284. Germanicus, statue in the Campana Museum, now in France.
285. Minerva, statue in the Campana Museum, now in France. This statue was formerly in the Giustiniani collection.
286. The Hermaphrodite, recumbent statue in the Campana Museum, now in Russia.
287. Antinous, statue in the Campana Museum, now in France.
288. Venus, statue in the Campana Museum, now in France.
289. Augustus, statue in the Campana Museum, now in Russia.
290.
* 291. The dying Gladiator, front view. Capitol.
* 292. The dying Gladiator, back view. Capitol.
* 293. The statue of Agrippina. Capitol.
* 294.
295.
296.
297. The Arch of Drusus.
* 298.
* 299. A Fountain, and Stone Pines, in the Villa Pamphilj-Doria.

* 300. The Piazza di Siena, in the Villa Borghese.
* 301. A Fountain with Sea Horses, in the Villa Borghese.
* 302.
303.
304. The Fish-Market in the Ghetto.
* 305. The Capitol from the Piazza of the Ara-Cœli.
306.
307. The Statue of Augustus in the Braccio nuovo of the Vatican discovered at Prima Porta 1863.
* 308.
* 309. Temples in the Forum, seen from the Mamertine prisons.
310. St. Peter, after the Fra Bartolomeo, in the Quirinal Palace.
311 St. Paul, after Fra Bartolomeo.
312. The Sleeping Faun, recumbent statue by Miss Hosmer.
* 313. Palace of the Cesars, from the Tarpeian Rock.
314. Hilda's Tower.
315.
316.
317. Isaac, front View.
318. Isaac, profile.
319. Indian Hunter-boy, and Fisher-girl.
320. Nydia fleeing from Pompei.
321. Ruth.
322. Angel of the Resurrection.
323. The Sentinel. } Rogers
* 324.
* 325.
326. Principal door-way of the Palazzo Comunale, Perugia.
* 327. Piazza del Duomo, Perugia.
* 328.
* 329. Statue of Pope Julius III, Perugia.
* 330.
* 331. Palazzo Publico, Gubbio.
* 332. Arch of Trajan, from the Arsenal, Ancona.
* 333. Port of Ancona.
* 334. Larger view of the Arch of Trajan. Ancona.
* 335. The Palazzo Farnese and church of St. Bridget.
* 336. The Palazzo Buonaparte, piazza di Venezia.
* 337. Piazza Navona, from the Palazzo Braschi.
* 338. General view of the Forum school of Xanthus in the foreground.
* 339. General view of the Forum of Trajan.
* 340.
* 341. Palace, church and baptistery of the Lateran.
* 342.
* 343. Fountain of Trevi.
344. Design of the Soldiers and Sailors Monument for the State of Rhode Island.
345. Design of the Soldiers and Sailors Monument, for the State of Michigan.
346. Bronze doors of the U. S. Capitol, Washington, executed by Randolph Rogers, Rome, and cast in bronze by F. v. Miller of Munich. } Rogers
347. The gilt bronze Hercules, found in the Theatre of Pompey.
* 348.
* 349. The Hall, of the Animals, Vatican.
* 350. The Gallery of Statues, Vatican.
* 351. The Protestant Cemetery within the walls of Rome.
* 352. View in the Island of Capri from the "Tregara".
* 353.
* 354.
* 355.
* 356.
* 357.
* 358.
* 359.
* 360.
* 361.
* 362.
* 363.
* 364. Porta St. Paolo with Pyramid of Cajus Cestius, as closed in 1867.
* 365.
* 366.
* 367.
* 368. Porta del Popolo as fortified in 1867.

(Contd.) *Catalogue of views by Macpherson, December 1871.*

* 369. The Muro Storto, with the barracks of the Pretorian Guard.
* 370.
* 371.
* 372. Ponte Nomentana.
* 373.
* 374.
* 375.
* 376.
* 377.
* 378.
* 379.
380. View on the Via Ostiensis, with the excavations at Ostia.
381. Near view of the Via Ostiensis, and the Castle of Ostia.
382. The Castle of Ostia.
383. Distant view of the Castle of Ostia.
384. General view of Ariccia with the viaduct.
385. Viaduct, and town of Ariccia on a larger scale.
386. Viaduct, and town of Ariccia, with Monte Gentili in the distance.
387. Nemi, from the Franciscan Convent.
388. Lake of Nemi, with Gensano in the distance.
389. Front view of the statue of President Lincoln, for the Pennsylvania monument, executed by Randolph Rogers.
390. Profile view of the statue of President Lincoln, by Rogers.
5... View in the Villa D'Este, Tivoli.
392. The Island of the Tiber.
393. Temple of Neptune.
394. Base of Column, Palace of the Caesars.
395. St. Lorenzo, outside the walls.

396. Sarcophagus.
397. Cupid and Psyche.
398. Venus of the Capitol.
399. Leda.
400. Mars, and Venus.
401. Innocence.
402. Antinous.
403. Faun.
404. Flora.
405. Isis.
406. Juno.
407. Amazon.
408. Apollo.
409. Zeno.
410. Marforio.
411. Julius Caesar.
412. The bronze Wolf.
413. Mars, reposing.
} Capitoline Museum.

414. Group of Gaul and Wife.
415. Head of Juno, on Altar.
416. Rape of Proserpine, Bernini.
417. Apollo.
418. Orestes and Electra.
419. Bacchus and Satyr.
420. Aristides, from Naples.
} Villa Ludovisi

* The numbers marked with an asterisk, indicate the subjects of a horizontal form.

In addition to the Photographs mentioned in this list, Mr. Macpherson has a volume of the choicest sculptures in the Vatican, the volume contains 134 Photographs, and is accompanied by a small volume of descriptive remarks The price of the volume is 150 francs. — There is just ready another volume containing all the interesting sculptures in the Capitoline Museum.

The volume contains 280 subjects, and the price of it is 300 francs. The photographs are sold separately at F. 1. 50.

(Contd.) *Catalogue of views by Macpherson, December 1871.*

ANCIENT ROME

N.B. Most of the photographs in this book have been taken from a large old album which bears on the title page the words: 'Macpherson's Photographs . Rome . 192. Via di Ripetta. 1858 Catalogue'. At the bottom right-hand corner of some of the photographs is a number written in ink which refers to the catalogue. These photographs are among the earliest of Macpherson's work, many of them dating back to 1853 or 1854. For this reason we have reproduced both the frontispiece and the catalogue, complete with the check marks in pencil made by the compiler of the album.

Authorship of the captions is indicated by the initials P.B. (Piero Becchetti) and C.P. (Carlo Pietrangeli).

THE COLOSSEUM

(1858 catalogue, no. 31 and 1863 catalogue, no. 32: 'The Coliseum on a smaller scale, with distant Latin and Alban mountains, and Church of St. John Lateran'; 28.3 × 40.2 cm; private collection.)

In the foreground are the walls of the Farnese gardens along the Via S. Bonaventura. Note the corner pavilion and gateway bearing the lilies of the Farnese coat of arms.
On the left are the top of the Arch of Titus, the podium of the Temple of Venus and Rome, and the *Meta Sudans*.
The Colosseum dominates the view and the inscription added in 1852 to commemorate the restoration work carried out under Pius IX is visible as a white square, left of centre.
On the right are the green slopes of the Caelian Hill, with the Altieri and Mellini vineyards and the Villa Casali. The cypress trees belong to the garden of the monastery of the Passionisti, nestling among the remains of the Temple of Deified Claudius.
In the background, from left to right, are: the campanile of S. Croce in Gerusalemme, the dome of SS. Pietro e Marcellino, the remains of the Neronian Aqueduct, the Sanctuary of the Scala Sancta and the monastery of the Passionisti (1852-56), the monastery of the SS. Quattro Coronati and, finally, the Lateran Palace and the Basilica of St. John Lateran, with its apse still intact.

C.P.

THE ARCH OF CONSTANTINE, FROM THE COLOSSEUM

(1858 catalogue, no. 3: 'Arch of Constantine north, facade, including the Meta Sudans, and a portion of the Convent of St. Bonaventura'; 29.2 × 39.7 cm; private collection.)

In 1805 excavations were carried out around the Arch of Costantine down to the ancient level. On the right is the *Meta Sudans*, which was cleared in 1743 and restored in 1934, only to be brutally demolished in 1936. The only ancient fountain left in the city, it is often referred to in ancient literature and also appears on many coins.

Behind, the Via di S. Gregorio, widened and lined with trees by Gregorio XVI in 1836, runs between the green slopes of the Caelian Park and the Palatine gardens.

C.P.

THE ARCH OF CONSTANTINE FROM THE VIA DI SAN GREGORIO

(1858 catalogue, no. 1: 'Arch of Constantine – south facade'; 26.9 × 38.4 cm; private collection.)

The Arch of Constantine seen from the south. In the background are some buildings used as haylofts and store rooms which overlook the Via del Colosseo near the junction with the Via della Polveriera.

C.P.

THE META SUDANS AND THE TEMPLE OF VENUS AND ROME

(1858 catalogue, no. 12. 'Temple of Venus and Rome, with distant view of the Roman Forum; taken from the Coliseum'; 28.7 × 38.9 cm; private collection.)

In the foreground is the fountain of the *Meta Sudans* on the road which leads up to the Arch of Titus. The arch was restored by Valadier in 1819-21, using travertine slabs. Valadier also restored the facade of the convent of S. Maria Nova (in 1810); the church itself is hidden by the ruins of the Temple of Venus and Rome, but the top of the Romanesque campanile is visible. In the background are the Capitoline Hill and one side of S. Maria in Aracoeli.

C.P.

THE META SUDANS AND THE TEMPLE OF VENUS AND ROME

(attributed to Macpherson, about 1860; 39.8 × 28.7 cm; private collection.)

On the left is the Arch of Constantine, half-hidden by one of the elm trees which Gregory XVI had planted along the Via S. Gregorio after the widening of the road in 1835. In front of it is the *Meta Sudans*, the only surving ancient Roman monumental fountain. It received its name from its resemblance to the conical turning post (*meta*) for chariot races in circuses, and from the fact that it 'sweated' water from the top and down the sides of the cone into a circular basin. The fountain was first restored in 1934 and then demolished in 1936.

C.P.

THE ARCH OF TITUS

(1858 catalogue, no. 27: 'Arch of Titus, Roman Forum'; 38.4 × 26.5 cm; private collection.)

The arch was restored in 1819-21 by Giuseppe Valadier, who replaced the damaged parts with travertine, to distinguish them from the marble of the original monument. The restoration is considered to be one of the best of its day. The road runs from the arch towards the Forum; note the well preserved basalt paving stones. In the background are the Temple of Antoninus and Faustina and the dome of the church of SS. Luca e Martina.

With typical Roman disregard, the residents of the neighbourhood have hung their washing out to dry on the low wall around the temple.   C.P.

ARCH OF TITUS – RELIEF DEPICTING A TRIUMPHAL PROCESSION

(1858 catalogue, no. 28: 'Bas-relief in the interior of the Arch of Titus, representing the procession of the seven-branched Candlestick'; 38.6 × 27.1 cm; private collection.)

One of the reliefs of the Arch of Titus, showing the triumphal procession of the Emperor after the conquest of Jerusalem.
The monument shows signs of neglect; apart from posters announcing the times of the services at local churches, there are some scribbles in charcoal and the inscription 'W. Santino Cianbelaro'. This inscription, which is probably centuries old, seems to refer to a local pastry vendor.

C.P.

VIEW OF ROME FROM THE PALATINE HILL TOWARDS THE QUIRINAL

(1858 catalogue, no. 149: 'View over Rome from the Palatine Hill'; 27.6 × 40.8 cm; private collection of P. Becchetti, Rome.)

The view was taken from the Palatine Hill. In the foreground is part of the Via Sacra, with newly-planted elm trees – the old ones had been removed in 1849 and were not replaced until 1855.
From left to right are the church of S. Lorenzo in Miranda (the Temple of Antoninus and Faustina), the convent and the church of SS. Cosma e Damiano (the Library of the Temple of Peace), with its rotonda dating from the time of Costantine in front (Temple of the Penates). Future excavations were to restore the ancient doorway, with its porphory columns, and the Roman bronze door, to their original level. The last structure on the right is the oratory of the Amanti di Gesù e Maria al Monte Calvario, the important brotherhood who used to organise the religious observances of the *Via Crucis* (Way of the Cross) in the Colosseum. The eighteenth century building was demolished in 1877.
Among the crowded tangle of houses it is possible to make out, going from left to right, the Villa Medici, the Colonna garden, the Quirinal Palace and tower, the Torre delle Milizie and the Torre del Grillo, the trees around the Villa Aldobrandini, the roof terrace of the Palazzo Rospigliosi, the convent of SS. Domenico e Sisto, the massive wall of the Forum of Augustus, the church of SS. Quirico e Giulitta with its Romanesque campanile, and the truncated Torre dei Conti rising up behind the campanile of SS. Cosma e Damiano.   C.P.

62

THE EXCAVATION OF THE BASILICA JULIA AND OF THE TEMPLE OF CASTOR

(1858 catalogue, no. 13: 'Excavations of the Julian Basilica, including a view of the various Temples in the Forum, with the Arch of Titus in the distance'; 38.3 × 27.1 cm; private collection.)

In the background are the Colosseum, the church of S. Maria Nova and the Arch of Titus. The trees along the Via Sacra have not yet been replanted after the removal of the previous ones in 1849. In the northern part of what is left of the ancient Campo Vaccino, a group of vegetable carts resists the advances of the archaeologists. A large ditch marks the limits of the excavations carried out in the middle of the century by Luigi Canina to unearth the podium of the Temple of Castor and the Basilica Julia, the floor and column-bases of which are visible in the foreground.

Behind the three surviving columns of the Temple of Castor is one of the corner pavilions of the wall that surrounded the Farnese Gardens; one end of the gateway designed by Girolamo Rainaldi, can be seen in profile. C.P.

THE GATEWAY TO THE FARNESE GARDENS AND THE CAPITOLINE

(1858 catalogue, no. 15: 'Forum Romanum – Looking towards the Capitol'; 29.6 × 39.8 cm; private collection.)

On the left is Girolamo Rainaldi's gateway to the Farnese Gardens, which was demolished in 1882 to make way for the excavation of the House of the Vestals. Further on are a few vegetable carts; behind them the excavations headed by Canina to unearth the podium of the Temple of Castor and the Basilica Julia are just beginning. The rows of small columns mark the excavation of the Column of Phocas, fenced off during the reign of Gregory XVI.

The Via Sacra, still without its trees, runs down from the top of the Velia towards the Arch of Septimius Severus.

The background is dominated by the stark rear facade of the Campidoglio; note the astronomical observatory on top of the Nicholas V tower, created in 1827 by Feliciano Scarpellini and enlarged in 1853 by Ignazio Calandrelli.

C.P.

THE CAPITOLINE FROM THE ROMAN FORUM

(1863 catalogue, no. 166: 'Julian Basilica, looking towards the Tabularium'; 30.2 × 39.7 cm; private collection P. Becchetti, Rome.)

In the foreground are the remains of the Basilica Julia, excavated by Canina in the middle of the century.

Behind is the Palazzo Senatorio and the Tabularium, only one arcade of which has been opened up, and beyond this the tower of Nicholas V with the Rome University astronomical observatory on the top. On the right is the monastery of S. Maria in Aracoeli.

C.P.

THE TEMPLE OF ANTONINUS AND FAUSTINA AND THE TEMPLE OF CASTOR

(1858 catalogue, no. 68: 'The three columns, formerly called the Temple of Jupiter Stator, and now styled Minerva Chalcidica, with the Temples of Peace, Antoninus and Faustina & c., in the Roman Forum; 28.7 × 37.5 cm; private collection.)

It may seem strange, but I prefer this view of the partially-buried Temple of Antoninus and Faustina, converted into a church by the architect Orazio Torriani, to the building itself. After the excavations, the exterior is neither temple nor church. Still, the centuries of continuous worship in the place cannot fail to be impressive, and in the photograph, the parts added in the seventeenth century seem to harmonise more successfully with the rest of the building than they do in real life.

Along the Via Sacra, where rope-makers no longer sit twisting their ropes, are the rotunda of SS. Cosma e Damiano (Temple of the Penates) and the oratory of the Amanti di Gesù e Maria al Monte Calvario. A barrier marks the limit of the excavation of the Temple of Castor (formerly thought to be the Temple of *Jupiter Stator*).

The campanile is that of SS. Cosma e Damiano (Library of the Temple of Peace); behind it are the enormous arcades of the Basilica of Constantine, (formerly believed to be the Temple of Peace).

C.P.

THE TEMPLE OF ANTONIUS AND FAUSTINA

(attributed to Macpherson, about 1860; 39.9 × 28.1 cm; private collection.)

A beautiful view of this stretch of the Via Sacra. From left to right: an old petrol street lamp at the beginning of the Via Maurina; the Temple of Antonius and Faustina (S. Lorenzo in Miranda), with the low barrier marking the extent of the excavations and the gateway onto the bridge to the church door; and lastly the Constantinian rotunda through which one passed to get to the church of SS. Cosma e Damiano from the Campo Vaccino.

Vegetable carts and wagons loaded with barrels and hampers add to the atmosphere of a 'rual metropolis' which Rome had not yet lost, and also provide a picturesque contrast with the majestic ruins and other surrounding buildings. Just a few years before this picture was taken, rope-makers were still at work along this part of the road.

C.P.

SIDE VIEW OF THE TEMPLE OF ANTONINUS AND FAUSTINA

(1858 catalogue, no. 21: 'Side view of the Temple dedicated to Antoninus and Faustina, Roman Forum'; 38.7 × 28.4 cm; private collection of P. Becchetti, Rome.)

The photographs shows one side of the Temple of Antoninus and Faustina, converted into the church of S. Lorenzo in Miranda (1601-1614).

The fact that the impressive columns are half-buried allows us a closer look at the frieze of fighting griffins which is under repair. Behind the Temple is the Via Maurina (named after Gregory XVI, Mauro Cappellari); the commemorative plaque states that the road was created in 1836 to allow the building to be seen from that side. The columns of the Temple have been excavated right down to their bases, and the site is protected by a barrier grille. Access to the church is by means of a bridge, like that at S. Angelo in Pescheria. In the background are the Arch of Septimius Severus and the Capitoline Hill, with the observatory on top of the Nicholas V tower.

C.P.

THE COLUMN OF PHOCAS AND THE TEMPLE OF SATURN

(1858 catalogue, no. 62: 'Phocas Column, Temple of Vespasian, Tabularium, etc.'; 28.1 × 38.2 cm; private collection.)

On the left is the Column of Phocas, excavated in 1813 and enclosed by a grille in 1835.

Behind is the Temple of Saturn and on the right the three columns of the Temple of Vespasian, also excavated and put back in position in 1813 by the French administration under the supervision of Giuseppe Camporese, who had constructed the carriage ramp up to the Capitoline in 1811. Camporese had transferred his services from the Pope (work in the Vatican Museum) to the French administration with no great upheaval.

C.P.

THE ROMAN FORUM FROM THE CAPITOLINE

(1858 catalogue, no. 16: 'Forum Romanum – General view taken from the Clivus Capitolinus, and including the principal Temples in the Forum, and the Arch of Titus'; 37.9 × 28.6 cm; private collection.)

Despite the grandeur of the ruins, this view is spoilt rather by the squalid surroundings. From among the gaping cavities of the excavations, the monuments of Ancient Rome rise up clean and stark, but of the green fields of the Campo Vaccino not even a single tree remains. In the foreground is the Temple of Saturn, and next to it the carriage ramp up to the Capitoline, built by the French. Behind are the three columns of the Temple of Castor and the church of S. Maria Liberatrice, which was demolished in 1900-1901 to make way for the excavation of S. Maria Antiqua. The Via Sacra (or, to be precise, the Stradone di Campo Vaccino), climbs gently up to the Arch of Titus. (Its trees, removed in 1849, have yet to be replaced). A line of vegetable carts is ranged up along the boundary of the excavation work; it seems almost as if the 'rural metropolis' is resisting the advances of the archaeologists, inch by inch. C.P.

THE COLUMN OF PHOCAS

(1858 catalogue, no. 89: 'Phocas' Column, excavated to the base'; 38.5 × 28.6 cm; private collection.)

The column of Phocas was excavated and re-erected in 1813 by the French administration; two years later it was surrounded by the barrier of bollards and iron St. Andrew's crosses which local residents found so useful for hanging out the washing. On the left is the Arch of Septimius Severus which was excavated under Pius VII in 1803; behind it is the the church of SS. Luca e Martina with its beautiful facade and dome by Pietro da Cortona; the Via Bonella runs between this church and that of S. Adriano, formerly the ancient *Curia Senatus*, or Senate House. On the right is an antiques shop which also sells photographs of Rome; the sign is in French to attract tourists. C.P.

THE TEMPLE OF SATURN

(1858 catalogue, no. 9: 'The eight Columns at the foot of the Capitol, formerly styled the Temple of Concord, and now the Temple of Vespasian or the Temple of Saturn'; 38.1 × 28.7 cm; private collection.)

This view shows the pronaos of the Temple of Saturn (formerly thought to be the Temple of Concord and the Temple of Vespasian); its huge fourth century columns rest on a podium which was constructed under Augustus. On the left are part of the facade and the campanile of S. Adriano (formerly the *Curia Senatus*).

C.P.

THE TEMPLE OF VESPASIAN

(attributed to Macpherson, about 1860; 40.1 × 29.7 cm; private collection.)

The three columns of the Temple of Vespasian (previously thought to be the Temple of *Jupiter Tonans*), were excavated and re-erected by the French administration under the direction of Giuseppe Camporese. On the left is the Palazzo Senatorio and tower of Nicholas V; in the background are the monastery of S. Giuseppe dei Falegnami and the steps from the Capitoline down to the Roman Forum. Washing hung out to dry in the sun has always been a trademark of the sunnier parts of the city – a fact which has never bothered the Romans, but which has earned Rome the title of 'the laundry capital' among tourists (Edmond About).   C.P.

THE ARCH OF SEPTIMIUS SEVERUS FROM THE ROMAN FORUM

(1858 catalogue, no. 111: 'Arch of Septimius Severus, looking from the Forum'; 27.4 × 38.2 cm; private collection.)

The Arch of Septimius Severus seen from the carriage ramp which leads up to the Capitoline. At one time the Via di Campo Vaccino used to pass right through the arch, but since the excavations under Pius VII, the monument has been surrounded by a ditch with a barrier at the top. The road now passes by to the right. Behind the arch it is possible to see the steps which lead down from the Campidoglio and pass by the church of S. Giuseppe dei Falegnami and the annexed oratory of the Crocifisso di Campo Vaccino.

The vegetable cart in the foreground, which is still covered up, is a clue to the time of day when the picture must have been taken.

C.P.

THE ARCH OF SEPTIMIUS SEVERUS SEEN FROM THE CAPITOLINE

(1858 catalogue, no. 66: 'The Arch of Septimius Severus, in the Roman Forum'; 39.1 × 28.7 cm; private collection.)

The Arch of Septimius Severus was excavated in 1803 by Giuseppe Camporese; there is a commemorative inscription on the retaining wall.
In the sunshine at the foot of the monument is a man whose pose seems to be the very personification of idleness.
Pietro da Cortona's facade of SS. Luca e Martina is just visible on the left hand side of the picture.

C.P.

THE VALLE MURCIA FROM THE PALATINE

(1858 catalogue, no. 110: 'Palace of the Caesars, on the Palatine'; size unknown; collection of Christie's, South Kensington, London).

An impressive and rare view of the *Circus Maximus* from the Palatine, with the ruins of the imperial palaces on the left. In the background are the Baths of Caracalla and behind them, on the horizon, the Aurelian Wall.
The tower on the right used to protect the church and convent of S. Balbina.
The Via dei Cerchi is lined, as it still is today, by large rustic buildings which hide the small church of S. Maria dei Cerchi.
In the middle of the Valle Murcia is the tower of the mill which used to belong to the Frangipane family; willow trees mark the course of the Acqua Mariana which flows through the valley to meet the Tiber near the present-day Ponte Palatino.

C.P.

THE ARCUS ARGENTARIORUM

(1858 catalogue, no. 76: 'Arch of the Goldsmiths, sometimes called the Little Arch of Septimius Severus, in the Forum Boarium'; 38.1 × 28.6 cm; private collection.)

This beautiful monument was erected in 203-204 in honour of the emperor Septimius Severus and his family by the moneychangers and cattle dealers who operated around the *Forum Boarium*. It is right next to the church of S. Giorgio al Velabro, of which the portico and the base of the campanile can be seen in the background. In 1870 part of the portico was demolished and set back in order to isolate the arch.

C.P.

THE BASILICA ULPIA AND TRAJAN'S COLUMN

(1858 catalogue, no. 20: 'Forum of Trajan'; 38.7 × 28.9 cm; private collection.)

In the foreground are Trajan's Forum and the columns of the Basilica Ulpia, unearthed by excavations carried out under Pietro Bianchi during the French administration. Behind the Basilica are Trajan's Column and the church of S. Maria di Loreto.

Behind Trajan's column is the palazzo (formerly Bonelli and Imperiali) which was bought by the banker, Vincenzo Valentini, at the end of the eighteenth century. In the nineteenth century, Valentini added another two storey building in a complementary style, designed by Filippo Navone and completed by G.B. Benedetti. This was finally finished in about 1840. The coat of arms on the facade was probably added at a time when the palazzo was used as a diplomatic residence; in 1874 the Portuguese Legation to the Quirinal had its headquarters there.

On the right one can just see the Sacristry of the SS. Nome di Maria, constructed by Giacomo Palazzi in 1839.

C.P.

THE BASE OF TRAJAN'S COLUMN

(1858 catalogue, no. 14: 'Base of the Column in the Forum of Trajan'; 39.7 × 26.2 cm; private collection.)

Macpherson's photographs are usually devoid of human figures in order to accentuate the solitary power of the monuments. This view of the base of Trajan's Column, in which the subtle play of light and shade throws the carvings into dramatic relief, is a rare exception. Just in front of the entrance is a seated man who, judging by the thick head of hair and long beard, must be Robert Macpherson himself. He obviously felt that this meditative pose would add to the impact of the photograph.

P.B.

THE CLOACA MAXIMA

(1858 catalogue, no. 154: 'The Cloaca Maxima'; 26.7 × 36.5 cm; private collection.)

Constructed in the second century B.C., the *Cloaca Maxima* is one of the oldest ancient Roman public works still in everyday use. Like most drains it was built underground, and is only visible at two points: where it enters the Tiber near the Ponte Rotto, and in the vicinity of the Arch of Janus. Until the end of the nineteenth century this last spot was one of the most picturesque places in Rome. Its atmosphere can be ascribed not only to the ivy-clad monument itself, as captured here by Macpherson, but also to the nearby spring used by a paper mill and by scores of women to do their washing.

Hans Christian Anderson, the great Danish fairy-tale writer, often used to stop at this spot during his stays in Rome. In his diary he wrote: '23 January 1834. Went to the Temple of Janus and saw the triumphal arch nearby. I then went down to the drain, crossing the half-collapsed arches. A peasant was washing his shoes in the clear blue water... and the ivy formed a leafy roof above him'.

In 1871 Orlando Jewitt used this picture to make an etching which was later used to illustrate Robert Burn's book, *Rome and the Campagna*.

P.B.

THE SO-CALLED 'TEMPLE OF MINERVA MEDICA'

(1858 catalogue, no. 24: 'Ruin called the Temple of Minerva Medica'; 23.2 × 38.3 cm; private collection.)

The nymphaeum of the Gardens of Licinius still goes by the incorrect name of the 'Temple of Minerva Medica' which was given to it by Pirro Ligorio. It was then part of the Villa of the Marchese Magnani, whose house can be seen on the right. Fruit trees and vegetable gardens give the scene a rural flavour.
In the background is the fourteenth century campanile of S. Maria Maggiore and the dome of the Borghese Chapel.

C.P.

THE ARCH OF DOLABELLA AND SILANUS

(1858 catalogue, no. 54: 'Arch of the Consul Dolabella on the Celian Hill'; 39.8 × 28.5 cm; private collection.)

The Arch of Dolabella and Silanus on the Caelian Hill, formerly the ancient *Porta Caelimontana* of the walls of Republican Rome. On top are the impressive remains of the Neronian Aqueduct which used to transport the Acqua Claudia to the Palatine.

Although it may not look like it, one can still pass through the arch; the wall in the background is that of the Garden of the Passionisti which passes close by S. Paolo della Croce. According to a story which dates back to the eighteenth century, St. John of Matha is supposed to have lived in two small rooms above the arch from 1209 to his death in 1213. This saint was the founder of the Trinitarians, the religious order which owned the nearby church and hospital of S. Tommaso *in formis*.   C.P.

MODERN ROME

PIAZZA DEL POPOLO

(1858 catalogue, no. 146: 'Piazza del Popolo, looking south'; 30.3 × 40 cm; private collection of P. Becchetti, Rome.)

Apart from the absence of traffic, this view has remained much the same; the only notable change is that the church of S. Maria in Montesanto has lost its weathercock.

The palazzo with the covered roof terrace in Via Ripetta is that of the Rondanini; its entrance is in the Via del Corso. Next to the fountain are a couple of barrel-carts used for cleaning the streets.

C.P.

THE OBELISK AND THE PORTA DEL POPOLO

(1858 catalogue, no. 94: 'The Piazza del Popolo, looking from the Corso'; 40.2 × 30 cm; private collection.)

The most notable difference between this photograph and the view today is that the Porta del Popolo still has the ashlar cladding which Valadier used on all the new buildings in the early decades of the nineteenth century in an attempt to unify the piazza. In 1879 the two side arches were opened up under the direction of the architect Agostino Mercandetti, who produced an elegant imitation of the sixteenth century architecture of the rest of the gateway.

The event was commemorated by inscriptions over the arches: one records that on the tenth anniversary of the city's newly-acquired liberty, the two lateral towers were demolished and the facade widened and restored; the other states that the Government constructed the two side arches to celebrate the growth of the Roman population since the restitution of the Eternal City to the rest of Italy.

C.P.

VIEW OF THE VATICAN FROM THE PINCIO

(1863 catalogue, no. 223: 'View over Rome, taking in the Vatican, from Monte Píncio'; 35.3 × 40.1 cm; collection of P. Becchetti, Rome.)

An unusual view of St. Peter's in the distance, with trees reflected in the still waters of the fountain in the foreground. In 1868 the marble sculpture of *Moses discovered in the Bullrushes* was placed in the middle of the fountain.
This had been carved by Ascanio di Brazzà, 'Conservatore' of Rome, and was later given to the City of Rome.   P.B.

THE VILLA MEDICI

(1858 catalogue, no. 25: 'The garden-front of the Villa Medici'; built from the design of Michael Angelo, on the Pincian Hill'; 27.9 × 37.8 cm; private collection.)

The photograph shows the garden facade of the Villa Medici, by Annibale Lippi, with its remarkable collection of antique marble sculptures which are still in place today. The only noticeable difference is that the two Egyptian lions have now been replaced by the copies of those at the Loggia dei Lanzi in Florence added in 1889.
The fountain in the middle of the courtyard is still missing its bronze copy of the statue of Mercury by Giambologna.

C.P.

THE TREVI FOUNTAIN

(1858 catalogue, no. 4: 'The Fountain of Trevi'; 41 × 31.4 cm; collection of P. Becchetti, Rome.)

This fountain is one of the most famous monuments of modern-day Rome. The best-known work of Nicola Salvi, it has always been admired as much for its architecture as for the gushing streams of water whose roaring fills the tiny piazza. With a slight degree of exaggeration, Madame de Staël wrote that whenever the fountain was not working, a great silence used to fall, not only on the piazza, but on the whole of Rome.

P.B.

THE PANTHEON

(1863 catalogue, no. 237: 'The Pantheon, from the Piazza della Rotonda'; 28.2 × 38.8 cm; private collection.)

The photograph shows the Pantheon still with the two bell-towers by Bernini, which were demolished in 1883.

On the right one can see the narrow passage between the Pantheon and the Palazzo Crescenzi, whose facade was knocked down and rebuilt further back during the excavation work.

The two lamps and the sign on the church door mean that the Holy Sacrament is on show. Near the fountain is a drinks stall.

C.P.

PIAZZA DELLA MINERVA

(attributed to Macpherson, about 1860; 39.1 × 32.2 cm; private collection.)

This elephant was designed in Bernini's workshop and carved by Ercole Ferrata to hold the small Egyptian obelisk from the sixth century B.C. which had formed part of the *Isaeum Campense* (or Temple of Isis) which formerly stood on the site of the piazza. The Domenican architect Giuseppe Paglia also had a part in the conception of this curious Baroque monument; the finished work was installed in 1667.

On the left is the seventeenth century building of the Accademia dei Nobili Ecclesiastici, formerly the Palazzo Severoli. Bought by Clement XI in 1706 as the headquarters of the body which trains young priests for the Holy See's diplomatic service, it is still known as the Pontificia Academia Ecclesiastica (Papal Ecclesiastic Academy). The facade was completely re-built by Gaetano Koch in about 1878.

To the side of the door is a salt and tobacco stall under a sign saying: 'Sale e tabacchi dell'Amministrazione cointeressata' ('Salt and tobacco co-operative').

In the background, up against the Pantheon, is the Palazzo Bianchi, with its beautiful corner balcony overlooking Piazza della Minerva. Formerly owned by the Vettori, Andosilla, Corsini and Palombara families, the palazzo was demolished in 1883 in order to isolate the Pantheon.   C.P.

FOUNTAIN IN THE GARDENS OF THE PALAZZO DI VENEZIA

(1858 catalogue, no. 98: 'The Fountain of the Doge, in the Cortile of the Venetian Palace'; 29.2 × 40.5 cm; private collection.)

In 1729 Carlo Monaldi received a commission from the Venetian Ambassador, Barbon Morosoni, for a fountain for the gardens of the Palazzo di Venezia; he had finished the work by 1730.
The central figure represents Venice throwing a ring into the sea in a gesture of power.
The photograph is interesting because it shows the fountain in what was presumably its original form, with two lions along the base and a small pillar in the middle, which are not there today. All that remains now is the central group and the surrounding *putti* holding shields which bear the names of the most celebrated victories of the Venetian Republic - Dalmatia, Candia, Morea and Cyprus.   C.P.

THE THEATRE OF MARCELLUS FROM THE PIAZZA MONTANARA

(1858 catalogue, no. 163: 'The Theatre of Marcellus, from the Piaza Montanara' 28.5 × 40.4 cm; collection of P. Becchetti, Rome.)

Piazza Montanara used to be one of the liveliest spots in nineteenth century Rome and was always packed with farm labourers in search of work. The northern end of the piazza was closed off by the Theatre of Marcellus, which had been transformed first into a fortress and later into a noble palazzo. The ground floor of the great arcade was occupied by craftsmen; in fact there were so many cork workshops that the street alongside the monument was named after them.   P.B.

THE CHURCH OF SANTA MARIA IN COSMEDIN

(1858 catalogue, no. 53: 'Church of Santa Maria in Cosmedin'; called the 'Bocca della Verità'; 39.9 × 28.7 cm; private collection.)

The ancient church of S. Maria in Cosmedin, founded in the fourth century, was given a new facade in 1718 on the order of Cardinal Annibale Albani. The fountain had been built a few years earlier, as part of the reorganisation of the piazza in front of the church under Clement XI (Albani 1700-1721); the architect was Carlo Francesco Bizzaccheri and the sculptor Francesco Moratti. The fountain fitted in very well, as the picture shows, but was altered during the much-discussed restoration of the church by G.B. Giovenale in 1894-5.

The campanile was restored in 1964 and the eighteenth century clock removed.   C.P.

THE 'TEMPLE OF VESTA' IN
THE FORUM BOARIUM

THE 'TEMPLE OF VESTA' IN
THE FORUM BOARIUM

(1858 catalogue, no. 17: 'Temple of
Vesta and the House of Rienzi';
40.3 × 29.7 cm; private collection.)

Apart from its careful composition, this view is of no particular interest; it shows the
two temples of the *Forum
Boarium* and, in the background, the house of the Crescenzi family. Excavations to
unearth the two podiums were
begun in 1832, in the area
between the temples marked
by the white bollards. The wall
of the Cenci gardens which
encroaches on the round temple has since been demolished.
C.P.

THE 'TEMPLE OF VESTA' AND THE FOUNTAIN IN THE PIAZZA BOCCA DELLA VERITÁ

(1858 catalogue, no. 19: 'Temple of Vesta and the Fountain, taken in summer'; 29.8 × 39.5 cm; private collection.)

The flattening effect which often occurs in old photographs is particularly pronounced in this view. On the left is the Garden of the Cenci and on the right the round temple of the *Forum Boarium*; the foreground is dominated by the Bizzaccheri fountain. To the right of the Temple are the metal girders of the footbridge imposed on the Ponte Rotto in 1853 to put it back into operation; on the left the facade of S. Salvatore *de pede pontis* can be seen at an angle. Later called SS. Crispino e Crispiniano, the church belonged to the order of the Calzolari, founded there by Leo XII in 1825. One of the characteristics of the church used to be its two small bell-towers on either side of the facade; it was demolished in 1884 to make way for the new embankment. The top of another bell-tower, just visible behind the gate of the Cenci Garden, must surely be that of S. Crisogono.
C.P.

THE 'SUMMER LAKE' IN PIAZZA NAVONA

(no. 49, untitled, in a printed list dated 1858; added in pencil is the title: 'Lago of Piazza Navona'. In the catalogue of 1863 another subject appears under no. 49; 32 × 41.5 cm; Texbraun collection, Paris.)

This remarkably sharp and bright photograph shows the Piazza Navona with its traditional 'summer lake' in the southern end of the square. This was made by blocking up the drains of the fountains and letting the water overflow into the piazza which, having no pavements, was shaped rather like a basin.

The practice went on until 1867. The dry part of the square was filled with market stalls selling all kinds of tools and utensils and there were many other shops in the buildings along that side of the square.

The Fontana del Moro in the foreground still has its original sculptures; these have since been substituted by copies – including 'Il Moro'. The originals now grace the Giardino del Lago in the Villa Borghese.

C.P.

FONTANA DEI QUATTRO FIUMI IN PIAZZA NAVONA

(1858 catalogue, no. 50: 'Base of the Obelisk and Fountain in the Piazza Navona'; 38.1 × 28.7 cm; private collection.)

The fountain is reflected in the waters of the summer 'lake' all around it. Behind is the church of S. Agnese in Agone, owned by the Pamphilj family, who rebuilt it in its present-day form next to their ancestral palazzo and the Collegio Pamphiliano for the education of future priests. The coat of arms in the centre of the facade is that of the the reigning Pope Pius IX (1846-78); on the left is that of the Roman People and on the right that of the Doria Pamphilj family (made up of the three branches Doria – Pamphilj – Landi, although from 1760 the Roman-Umbrian branch of the Pamphilj died out, leaving only the Doria-Landi branch from Genoa). The coat of arms of the Roman People features a votive chalice and four candles, the traditional gift to the church from the City Magistrates on the feast of S. Agnese every other year on 21 January. Note that the gate in front of the church, designed by Andrea Busiri Vici in 1853, has yet to be installed.

C.P.

THE FORUM OF NERVA

(1858 catalogue, no. 5: 'A portion of the Forum of Nerva, sometimes called the Temple of Pallas'; 40.5 × 31.5 cm; collection of P. Becchetti, Rome.)

Detail of the precinct wall of the Forum of Nerva and the two enormous Corinthian columns ('Colonnacce') before the excavations. The most interesting thing to notice is the entrance to the old bakery, with all the loaves and prices on display above the door exposed to the sund and dust. The sign says: 'Ant(ico) Forno Casareccio. Spaccio di tutte sorti. Generi Commestibili' ('Old Home-Cooking Bakery. All kinds of goods and general groceries').
This old bakery nestling in the ruins is a typical example of the extraordinary contrasts which visitors to Rome found so appealing. As Nicholas Hawthorne commented on this bakery: 'The ruins of a great and almost divine past are not above providing for our humble, everyday needs'.

C.P.

THE ARCH OF THE PANTANI AND THE COLUMNS OF THE TEMPLE OF MARS ULTOR

(1858 catalogue, no. 7: 'Columns of the Forum of Nerva, and the Arch called 'L'Arco dei Pantani'; 40.3 × 30.1 cm; private collection.)

A beautiful clear view of the Arch of the Pantani in the ashlar precinct wall of the Forum of Augustus, with the three columns of the Temple of *Mars Ultor* in the background. The columns have already been excavated and enclosed by railings, and the lovely Romanesque campanile of S. Basilio which used to encroach on the site has been demolished, in spite of Stendhal's protests.

On the corner of the Via Baccina is a much-frequented shrine where pipers can often be seen playing in nineteenth century views of Rome. It would certainly be hard to find a more impressive back-drop. The splendid tabernacle and canopy have since vanished. Note the petroleum street lamp on the left.

C.P.

101

THE FONTANA DEL TRITONE

(not included in Macpherson's catalogues, but almost certainly taken by him; 27.9 × 39.2 cm; private collection.)

This photograph of the Fontana del Tritone in summer is a typical example of Macpherson's sensitivity as a photographer. The viewpoint is almost the same as that taken in winter (opposite), but the time of day must have been different as the shadows are shorter. Along the Via dei Cappuccini the elm trees are in full bloom; these were later to provide the inspiration for one of Gabriele D'Annunzio's best-known poems.

P.B.

THE FONTANA DEL TRITONE IN WINTER

(1858 catalogue, no. 40: 'Fountain of the Piazza Barberini taken in winter'; 27.7 × 39.1 cm; private collection.)

Piazza Barberini has always been one of the coldest and windiest spots in Rome. Quite often in winter the muscular figure of the sea-god is completely covered in frost and fantastic icicles. Even though some of the ice has been broken off and smashed at the bottom of the picture, one is reminded of the sonnet by Belli written on 7 February 1833: '*E annate a vede un po' che bagattella/ 'De zazzera c'ha messo Tiritone*' . Behind is the Capuchin monastery and its elm trees, now all bare. The cross in front of the building has since been transferred to Centocelle – its base was created out of an old *cipollino* column by Thorvaldsen, who had his studios in the piazza and used to live in what is now the Via Sistina.

P.B.

THE 'SPANISH STEPS' AND CHURCH OF TRINITÁ DEI MONTI

(1858 catalogue, no. 51: 'Church of the Trinità de' Monti'; 29.6 × 38 cm; private collection.)

The photograph shows the eighteenth century steps by Francesco De Sanctis (1723-26) leading up to the church of Trinità dei Monti, which are in a rather bad state of disrepair. The wild areas on either side are now private gardens. The large stucco coat of arms of Louis XVIII supported by angels in the centre of the facade had been added during the restoration work by Mazois and was removed in 1871.

C.P.

BALUSTRADE OF THE CAMPIDOGLIO AND THE BASILICA OF SANTA MARIA IN ARACOELI

(1858 catalogue, no. 148: 'Horses of the Capitol, from the Piazza Caffarelli'; 40.2 × 29.8 cm; private collection.)

In this picture the Dioscuri and other sculptures around the Capitol are badly blackened and rain-damaged. It is interesting to note that the balustrade by Giacomo Della Porta is still clearly visible before being buried during work on the Via delle Tre Pile in 1872. On the retaining wall of the steps up to S. Maria in Aracoeli is a commemorative tablet (now hidden by vegetation) recording the visit by the Austrian Emperor, Francesco I, in 1819.

On the facade of the church is the dial of the eighteenth century clock (1728) which was removed in 1806, when the famous clock of the Roman People was placed on top of the Capitoline tower. The side of the church bears signs of the restoration work carried out – the date 1851 has been scrawled in chalk by the builders, together with the initials L.A. 'fescit' (fecit), in perfect 'Latinese'.

C.P.

105

VIEW FROM THE PIAZZA DEL CAMPIDOGLIO

(attributed to Macpherson, around 1860; 27.2 × 39.6 cm; private collection.)

The foreground of this view has hardly altered, but the buldings in the distance have undergone some changes. The houses at the bottom of the stairs, in what was the Piazza Aracoeli, no longer exist; the one with the covered roof-terrace is the Palazzo Santacroce (later De Romanis and De Rossi) which was demolished in 1929.
The houses along the Scalinata d'Aracoeli are no longer standing either, and one can just make out the roof of the church of S. Rita which faces into the Via Giulio Romano.

C.P.

EQUESTRIAN STATUE OF MARCUS AURELIUS

(1858 catalogue, no. 29: 'Equestrian bronze statue of Marcus Aurelius,
standing in the square of the Capitol'; 40.1 × 30.2 cm; private collection).

In the centre of the Piazza del Campidoglio is the equestrian statue of Marcus Aurelius by Michelangelo, installed there in 1537 on the magnificent base which he also designed. The bronze still has a beautiful black shine which it has completely lost over the last few decades. The small columns around the statue were part of the original design; they were removed in 1940 when the star design of the payment was restored by Antonio Muños.

C.P.

THE CHURCH OF SANTA PUDENZIANA

(1858 catalogue, no. 65: 'Church of Santa Pudenziana, the titular church of Cardinal Wiseman'; 39.5 × 29.3 cm; private collection.)

This photograph must surely be a tribute by the Catholic Macpherson to Cardinal Nicholas Patrick Wiseman, the titular priest of this great old church. He was the first British cardinal to be appointed after the restoration of the ecclesiastical hierarchy by Pius IX. Rector of the English College in Rome, Wiseman (1802-1865) was a well-known figure in Italy. He was created a Cardinal on 30 September 1850 and died in London on 15 February 1865. The photograph shows only the tall Romanesque campanile and part of the church. Two marble candelabras and the mount supporting the cross disappeared during restoration work carried out on the facade in 1870 by Antonio Manno for Cardinal Lucian Bonaparte. The tympanum was also altered, with a fresco by Pietro Gagliardi of the Redeemer worshipped by angels replacing the previous decoration. The central window, of which just the top is visible here, was closed up and replaced by two smaller windows, and instead of the old entrance, monumental steps were built up to the new door. The adjacent buildings along the Via Urbana were also either knocked down or altered at this time. On the left is the enormous Palazzo Cimarra, converted into a barracks in the early 1800s and still in operation today. At the bottom left hand corner of the photograph is the coat of arms of Cardinal Wiseman.

P.B.

PIAZZA SANTA MARIA MAGGIORE

(1858 catalogue, no. 43: 'Church of Santa Maria Maggiore'; 29 × 39.4 cm; private collection.)

This rather damaged photograph shows the Piazza S. Maria Maggiore before the reorganisation of the roads around the basilica in 1870 lifted the church up above the rest of the square. The gateway of S. Antonio Abate, the ancient entrance to the Hospital of the Antoniani on the left, can still be reached from the road, without the huge double stairway constructed in about 1875.

On the left is the column commemorating the conversion of Henry IV of France, which has since been moved to the side of S. Maria Maggiore.

To the right of S. Antonio is the Hospital of the Antoniani, rebuilt by Pius IV (1559-1565); this is under restoration, as shown by the beams of the scaffolding protruding from the walls.

The campanile of S. Maria Maggiore still has its original fifteenth century clockface with six numbers; this has since been removed, together with the square mount.

C.P.

VIEW FROM PIAZZA SAN PIETRO IN VINCOLI

(attributed to Macpherson, about 1860; 28.5 × 37.9 cm; private collection.)

The Piazza San Pietro in Vincoli has changed a lot since this picture was taken; it is now blocked off at the end by modern buildings which deprive it of the airiness of earlier times. At one time the Via di S. Pietro in Vincoli used to lead down from the Margani tower (which was begun in the twelfth century, completed in the fifteenth century and later reduced to just the campanile of S. Francesco di Paola) to the Basilica of Maxentius; this route has now been interrupted by the big walls of the Via degli Annibaldi.

The palm tree in the middle is one of the typical motifs of these nineteenth century views; indeed, they are one of the most picturesque elements in the Roman landscape.

The view includes the dome of SS. Luca e Martina and the Capitoline in the background; the statue of 'Christian Rome' (an ancient statue of Artemis, since removed) which from 1582 used to sit on top of the Capitoline tower, must have been erased by Macpherson when he was touching up the sky.

C.P.

THE QUIRINAL HILL WITH FOUNTAIN AND OBELISK

(attributed to Macpherson, even though his stamp is missing. See 1858 catalogue, no. 96: 'The Quirinal Hill with the Obelisk and Horses'; 30.1 × 40.6 cm; private collection.)

The photograph shows the famous group of the Dioscuri (Castor and Pollux) on either side of the obelisk installed by Giovanni Antinori at the time of Pius VI, and the circular fountain added in 1818 by Pius VII to replace the previous fifteenth century one.

The coach-houses on the right were demolished during Vespignani's transformation of the piazza in 1866, and the stables, begun by Fuga and completed by Alessandro Specchi (1722-1730), were also greatly altered. The small eighteenth century porch for the guardsmen, just visible to the left of the picture, was demolished during this work.

C.P.

111

CYPRESS TREES IN THE CLOISTERS OF SANTA MARIA DEGLI ANGELI

(1858 catalogue, no. 64: 'Cypresses planted by Michael Angelo in the Cloisters of Santa Maria degli Angeli'; 39.1 × 27.6 cm; private collection.)

The cloister was built in 1565, as is confirmed by the inscription on one of the corner pilasters near the entrance. This was the year before the death of Michelangelo, who is supposed to have designed the building; it is more likely, however, to be the work of Jacopo del Duca. Tradition has it that the group of huge cypresses in the foreground, which are still flourishing, were planted by Michelangelo himself. The neat vegetable garden is quite in line with the Rule of the Certosini, but rather at odds with the architecture of the cloister.

P.B.

THE PORTA SAN LORENZO

(1858 catalogue, no. 158: 'Porta San Lorenzo, 29.5 × 39.9 cm; private collection.)

The view shows the inner door of the Porta S. Lorenzo, which was demolished in 1869. Note the street lamp and sentry box. Further back is the lower door or ancient *fornix* of the aqueduct of the Aquae Marcia, Tepula and Julia. The towers of the ancient Roman gate were replaced by sixteenth century ones which bear the coats of arms of Cardinal Antonio Carafa and Alessandro Farnese (1584). On the left is the elegant eighteenth century customs house, similar to the one still standing today at Porta S. Paolo; note the shrine between the windows and the stars over the lintels, which probably allude to the reign of Pope Clement XI (1700-1721).

On the lower walls are various types of scales with which the customs officers used to weigh all the goods being taken into the city.

C.P.

THE 'ARCH OF SIXTUS V'

(atributed to Macpherson, about 1860; 38.7 × 27.9 cm; private collection.)

On the right are the City Walls, and in the background the travertine and *peperino* 'Arch of Sixtus V', erected in 1585 and 1586 to carry the Acqua Felice along the new route created by the pope to his villa (now the Via Marsala). This new road is mentioned on the arch, together with the Via di Porta S. Lorenzo which used to skirt around the Villa Peretti on its way to S. Maria Maggiore. The road has since disappeared during the construction of the residential quarter at Esquilinio; its old route would have sliced diagonally through the new development. The photograph shows the little piazza where this road finished up, near the Porta S. Lorenzo.

C.P.

VIEW OF TRASTEVERE AND THE AVENTINE FROM THE JANICULUM

(1858 catalogue, no. 100: View of the Alban Mountains from the Church of San Pietro in Montorio; 27.4 × 37.9 cm; private collection.)

High up on the left hand side are the church and convent of S. Sabina and the church of SS. Alessio e Bonifacio, with its tall Romanesque campanile. In the centre is the complex of buildings making up S. Maria del Priorato, whose facade had been deprived of its Piranesi pediments in 1849, during the seige of Rome by the French artillery under General Oudinot. Almost on alignment with the church's piazza is the loggia of San Saba.

On the same level, but further to the right, is the 'Colonnella' or Farnese fortress, which overlooks Monte Testaccio. The long building of the Ospizio Apostolico di S. Michele and the upper part of the facade of S. Francesco a Ripa stretch across the middle of the picture. In the foreground is the Trastevere district, with its cottages and gardens destroyed by the development of the area in 1870.

P.B.

PYRAMID OF CAIUS CESTIUS AND THE PROTESTANT CEMETERY

(1858 catalogue, no. 128: 'Pyramid of Caius Cestius, and the English Burying-ground'; 29.6 × 38.8 cm; private collection.)

The photograph shows the pyramidal tomb of the *praetor*, Caius Cestius, inserted into the Aurelian Wall. The trees on the left form part of the Protestant (or English) cemetery; this had been founded at the end of the eighteenth century, but underwent rapid development in the early decades of the nineteenth. Its immaculate maintenance today provides a sharp contrast with the neglect in evidence in this picture.

C.P.

THE PROTESTANT CEMETERY AT TESTACCIO

(not included in Macpherson's catalogues, but bears his stamp – n. 15; 14 × 23.2 cm; collection of P. Becchetti, Rome.)

The Protestant Cemetery is without doubt one of the most interesting places in Rome. Watched over by the enormous pyramidal tomb of Caius Cestius, the cemetery always makes a deep impression on visitors, both for the simple beauty of its setting, and for the memories it conjures up of all those buried there. Artists and poets from all over the world have been inspired by this peaceful green oasis.

In the foreground, on the other side of the wall, is the tomb of the English poet, John Keats, who died in Rome, in the Piazza di Spagna, on 24 February 1821. A similar tombstone was erected next to it in 1879 – that of his great friend, Joseph Severn, a painter and British Consul in Rome for over a decade.

P.B.

THE PORTA MAGGIORE

(1858 catalogue, no. 26: 'The Porta Maggiore, and Tomb of the Baker'; 30.1 × 40.6 cm; private collection.)

There were two arches in the monumental aqueduct built by Claudius in A.D. 52; through them passed the Via Prenestina and the Via Labicana. When the aqueduct was made part of the Aurelian Wall, these two arches became gateways into the city. The Porta Labicana was closed soon afterwards, but the Porta Prenestina remained open and was fortified over the centuries. In 1837, following the completion of the excavations at the Roman Forum, the pope's work force was transferred to the Porta Maggiore; they demolished the other door and tore down the towers, including that built by Nicholas V, which had been put up to protect the gate.

During this demolition work, the tomb of the baker Eurysaces was discovered in 1838. Finally the two arches were partially closed by battlemented walls, leaving only the Porta Prenestina in operation.

The excavation of the surrounding land uncovered the monuments down to their original level. The work was finished in 1841.

C.P.

THE VILLA PAMPHILJ – VIEW OF THE GARDENS

(1858 catalogue, no. 69: 'View of the Lake in the Villa Doria' 28.5 × 38.4 cm; private collection.)

A view of the gardens as they appeared in the nineteenth century, with the statues and cascades leading down to the lake created from the seventeenth century oval fishpond.

In the background is the Fontana del Giglio; then comes a facade punctuated by statues in niches and then the stream and cascades, with various sculptures dotted along the banks. Today, nothing remains of this but the memory; the lake has dried up, the stream is a smelly ditch, the statues have all disappeared and the background of the view is filled with modern buildings which now crowd in on the villa from all sides.

C.P.

VIEW OF ROME FROM THE SLOPES OF MONTE MARIO

(attributed to Macpherson, around 1858; 22.1 × 39.4 cm; private collection.)

On the right in the foreground are the Castel S. Angelo and the Prati di Castello, with no houses to be seen.

The most important element is the Villa Altoviti in front of the Palazzo Borghese; it appears as a white block surrounded by trees. In the background, from left to right, one can make out the Villa Medici, the church of Trinità dei Monti, the dome of S. Carlo al Corso (with the smaller one of S. Rocco in front), the church of S. Girolamo degli Schiavoni, the Palazzo Borghese and the Quirinal Hill, with the campanile of S. Maria Maggiore rising up behind.

C.P.

PANORAMA OF MONTE MARIO AND THE VILLA MELLINI

(not included in any of Macpherson's catalogues, but attributed to him, about 1865; 11.4 × 14.3 cm; collection of P. Becchetti, Rome.)

Towards the left, along the profile of the hill, is the famous pine tree of Monte Mario, saved from the axe in 1821 by Sir George Beaumont, who bought it and then donated it to the City of Rome. William Wordsworth wrote a sonnet about this tree when he returned to England in 1837 after a trip to Rome.

It had also been the subject of some sketches by the famous Danish writer Hans Christian Anderson, but was finally felled in 1909.

P.B.

121

VIEW OF ROME FROM THE JANICULUM

(attributed to Macpherson, about 1860; 29.4 × 40.2 cm; private collection.)

This photograph was taken from the top of the Janiculum. In the foreground are the Palazzo Corsini and its riding stables, before they were invaded by vegetation. The mass of buildings jutting out in the centre marks the road (nowadays interrupted by other streets), which used to lead to the 'scala d'acqua' in the Villa Riario. Notice the little houses along the Via dei Riari and the Via della Penitenza on the left, with their gardens at the back. The building on the corner of the Via della Lungara and the Via della Penitenza is the Istituto del Buon Pastore, which includes the church of S. Croce delle Scalette.

In the foreground is the Tiber, with houses lining its banks.

Behind the Palazzo Corsini, on the other side of the Tiber, is the Palazzo Falconieri with its loggia by Borromini; then come the Palazzo Farnese, the dome of S. Andrea della Valle and the Quirinal. Behind the facade of S. Caterina dei Senesi are the Palazzo della Cancelleria and the Pantheon. Pushing up between the rooftops are the campanile of S. Ivo alla Sapienza and the tower of S. Andrea delle Fratte, both by Borromini. Further to the left are the dome and campanile of S. Agnese in Agone and Trinità dei Monti in the distance; on the extreme left are the facade of the Chiesa Nuova, the dome of S. Carlo al Corso and the Villa Medici.   C.P.

THE VILLA RIARIO-CORSINI

(attributed to Macpherson, about 1860; 30.6 × 41.2 cm; private collection.)

The railings in the foreground form part of the work done on the Palazzo Corsini and the surrounding area by Ferdinando Fuga from 1736 onwards. The riding stables he created have since been turned into gardens.

The villa behind the railings has since been taken over by the Botanic Gardens, without preserving any of its original features. At the time the picture was taken, it was still the sixteenth century Villa Riario, attached to the palazzo of the Riario family and later bought by the Corsini. The villa was set among small lanes and waterfalls on the slopes of the Janiculum. This winter-time view shows one axis of the villa terminating in a niche with a piece of ancient statuary. A niche like this one survives today in a wooded part of the Janiculum beneath the Promenade, completely abandoned

and separated from its original setting.

On the top of the hill is the *casino* Riario which has since been demolished; it used to stand where the big canon is now. Queen Christina of Sweden lived here for a time, while repairs were being carried out to the Palazzo Riario – her home until she died. In 1736 the *casino* and other property on the Janiculum was sold by the Riario Sforza family to the Corsini, who in turn donated it all to the State in 1883. The *casino* was demolished in about 1895, when the monument to Garibaldi was erected. The Botanical Gardens were moved there later (in 1888 they were still in the Via Panisperna); while the upper part was designated the 'Promenade of the Janiculum' by the State and was opened to the public at the end of 1887.   C.P.

PANORAMA OF ROME FROM THE JANICULM

(attributed to Macpherson, about 1857; 26.3 × 38.4 cm; private collection.)

On the horizon, up on the left, one can just make out some wooden structures on the Piazzale del Pincio; these must be the supports of the famous Catherine wheel which used to be burned there. Moving on towards the right, one can see the dome of S. Agnese, the Palazzo Farnese and its loggia by Giacomo Della Torre, the dome of S. Carlo al Corso, the Villa Medici, the church of S. Ivo, the church of SS. Trinità dei Monti and the domes of SS. Trinità dei Pellegrini and S. Carlo ai Catinari. Far behind are the pine trees of the Villa Borghese and the Villa Ludovisi. And below, in the foreground, are the convent and campanile of S. Egidio in Trastevere and the tall building of the Palazzo Velli.

P.B.

THE TIBER

VIEW OF THE TIBER, CASTEL SANT'ANGELO AND ST. PETER'S

(1858 catalogue, no. 34: 'The Castle and Bridge of St. Angelo, with the Vatican in the distance'; 25.7 × 38.3 cm; private collection.)

Taken from quite high up, this view focuses on the Castle and St. Peter's rather than on the river, which does not take up as much of the picture. It must be one of the earliest photographs of the Tiber taken by Macpherson; it can be dated about 1855 or earlier, because work has not yet begun on the Piazza Pia, later created and named in honour of Pope Pius on the other side of the Ponte S. Angelo.

P.B.

VIEW OF THE TIBER, CASTEL SANT'ANGELO AND ST. PETER'S

(1858 catalogue, no. 34: 'The Castle and Bridge of St. Angelo, with the Vatican in the distance'; 21.7 × 38.3 cm; collection of P. Becchetti, Rome.)

Although this view also carries the number 34 in pencil on the dry stamp, it is very different from the earlier photograph. Not only does it take in a far broader area, from the piazza by the bridge to the Nicchione del Belvedere; it must also have been taken at least three years later. Behind the entrance to the Castle one can see one of the twin buildings in the new Piazza Pia; the other was completed by 1861, when the piazza was officially opened.

P.B.

CASTEL SANT'ANGELO SEEN FROM THE CASA BONADIES IN THE PIAZZA DI PONTE

(1858 catalogue, no. 35: 'The Castle of St. Angelo, on a larger scale' 30.5 × 36.4 cm; collection of P. Becchetti Rome.)

The Piazza di Ponte in the foreground was one of the busiest traffic spots in the city, because it gave access to St. Peter's. It was also a place with rather sinister associations, on account of the frequent executions carried out there. The last one occurred on 27 July 1841, when three people were put to death for 'theft and the pre-meditated murder of Caterina Iachizzi, wife of Francesco Iachizzi, a watch-maker in the Offices of the Vicariate'. During the lengthening of the Ponte S. Angelo in 1893, the statues of the apostles (of which only Peter is visible in the picture) were removed and remounted, but this was done wrongly, so that the inscription pointed in towards the bridge and the papal crest towards the piazza. To the right of the bridge is the old entrance to the Castle; this was demolished during the widening of the river, but was reconstructed in 1926 in the side of the castle.

P.B.

130

VIEW OF THE TIBER FROM THE JANICULUM

(attributed to Macpherson, about 1856; 22 × 38.9 cm; private collection.)

This is a very unusual view of Rome and the Tiber taken from the Janiculum. The eye travels from the Pincio on the far left, where the arcades by Valadier can be seen leading to the church of Trinità dei Monti and beyond. It is a surprise to see the whole of the Ponte S. Angelo, and its junction with the Castle protected by a large iron cage-like structure. Behind this is the large expanse of the Villa Altoviti which would later be hidden by the Palazzo di Giustizia, The Tiber seems almost like a lake from this angle and the bend at the Tor di Nona is completely surrounded by houses which drop down sheer to the water. The imposing building on the left hand side of the foreground is the Hospital of Santo Spirito. The horizon is dotted by the pine trees of the Villa Borghese and the Villa Ludovisi, which have inspired so many writers and poets.

P.B.

PANORAMA OF THE TIBER AND THE AVENTINE FROM THE CAPITOLINE

(1858 catalogue, no. 56: 'View of the Aventine from the Tarpeian Rock; 26.9 × 37.8 cm; private collection.)

The upper part of the picture shows the Aventine Hill, with the churches of S. Sabina, S. Alessio e Bonifacio and S. Maria del Priorato clinging to its slopes. Down below is the Tiber; on the Aventine side one can see a floating mill anchored to one of the ancient piers of the *Pons Sublicius*. On the other pier, the slow turning of a *giornello* (rotating fishing rod) has created a 'ghost' in the photograph, on account of the long exposure time. In the bottom left hand corner is the small dome of the church of S. Omobono, the patron saint of tailors. The rather intrusive dates scrawled in chalk on a wall indicate the years in which restoration work was carried out. On the extreme right is the massive building of the Ospizio Apostolico di San Michele, and its enormous clock in one of the courtyards.

P.B.

133

THE PONTE ROTTO FROM THE AVENTINE

(1858 catalogue, no. 22: 'View of the 'Ponte Rotto' with the new Suspension Bridge'; 27.4 × 39.7 cm; private collection.)

The Ponte Rotto – the ancient *Pons Aemilius*, is seen here when it was connected to the Bocca della Verità by the iron suspension bridge constructed in 1853 by the firm Braschi and Co. Pius IX himself wanted to be the first to cross it, in his carriage with all the papal court behind him, on 29 September.
In 1871, the government technical commission, appointed after the disastrous floods of 28 December 1870, ruled that all structures which in any way impeded the flow of the river should be pulled down. This included the Ponte Rotto, of which only the last arch remains, like an island in the middle of the river.

P.B.

134

VIEW OF THE CLOACA MAXIMA AND THE 'TEMPLE OF VESTA'

(1858 catalogue, no. 67: 'View of the Cloaca Maxima, Temple of Vesta, Church of the Bocca della Verità, etc.; three slightly different views exist under this number, all attributed to Macpherson, but taken at different times; 29 × 39.6 cm; private collection.)

From the top left are: the ruins of the Palatine; the 'Temple of Vesta' with the chimney of the 1853 gasworks at the *Circus Maximus* sticking up behind; the wide Baroque facade of S. Maria in Cosmedin, ill-advisably torn down in 1893, and the tall Romanesque campanile with its huge clock, also since removed. In the centre are the trees and pergolas of the garden of the Cenci, which used to stretch down to the river here, and further down is the mouth of the *Cloaca Maxima*, one of the hydraulic masterpieces of the Roman Republic.

Another opening can be seen further along to the right. This is the outlet of the ancient Acqua Mariana, diverted in 1125 on the orders of Pope Callisto II to supply water to all the flour mills of the city. The construction of the high embankments means that the buildings in the Piazza di Bocca della Verità are not only further away from the river now, but they also appear to be lower down.

The *Cloaca Maxima* has been very well-preserved, but the ancient outlet of the Acqua Mariana is hardly visible in the thick wall.

P.B.

VIEW OF THE TIBER AND THE CAPITOLINE FROM THE MARMORATA

(1858 catalogue, no. 55: 'View of the Capitoline Hill, from the foot of the Aventine'; 26 × 37.8 cm; private collection.)

Macpherson took many photographs of this stretch of the Tiber. At his time it was one of the most historically interesting parts of the river, and it was also very picturesque. On the left is part of the Casino di Donna Olimpia, with its gardens supported by an enormous retaining wall; behind it is the metal suspension bridge of the Ponte Rotto. The tall campanile of the Capitoline and the medieval Torre delle Milizie rise up in the centre, and on the right, the campanile of S. Maria in Cosmedin is just visible above the rooftops.

The real subject of the view is the Tiber. In the centre are the remains of the piers of the ancient *Pons Sublicius*, with a floating mill snchored to one of them. This was the mill of San Mauro, owned by the Principe Torlonia and used for grinding salt from the salt mines at Ostia and Corneto (Tarquinia). In 1857 it was sold and transferred to the Tiber Island, where it replaced the mill of Santa Maria in Fontana, which had sunk two years previously. On the Aventine bank is an old bare tree known as the 'miseria', a large lantern and a sentry box used as a shelter by the customs officers. The creation of the embankments brought many changes. Even the remains of the *Pons Sublicius* had to be blown up with dynamite because, according to the technical commission appointed after the floods in December 1870, they impeded the flow of the river.

P.B.

VIEW OF THE TIBER FROM THE MARMORATA

(1858 catalogue, no. 55: 'View of Capitoline Hill from the foot of the Aventine'; 28.8 × 40.2 cm; private collection.)

Although it bears the same number, this photograph is quite different from the one taken further downstream. This picture includes the warehouses built by Gregory XVI at the Port of Ripa Grande, just visible on the left. And, since it was taken several years later, the mill which was previously anchored to the pier of the *Pons Sublicius* has been moved to the Tiber Island. The campanile of S. Maria in Cosmedin appears slightly smaller in this picture, as part of it was lost during Macpherson's work on the sky.

P.B.

THE VATICAN

THE FACADE AND LEFT SIDE OF THE VATICAN BASILICA

(1858 catalogue, no. 58: 'St. Peter's from the Janiculum Hill'; 29.8 × 40.1 cm; private collection.)

This view was taken from the Monte San Spirito. At the foot of the hill are the brickyards which gave the church of S. Maria delle Fornaci its name, separated from the Vatican by the City Walls around the Porta Fabbrica. Inside the walls, on the left, are the Palazzo del S. Ufficio (Holy Office), the small church of S. Maria in Camposanto with its Germanic cemetery, and the Sacristry and Canonry of St. Peter's, to which the house for the Beneficiati has yet to be added (1864). The map drawn up by the Census of 1866 shows an iron foundry near the Palazzo del S. Ufficio. The Porta Cavalleggeri is hidden by the slopes of Monte S. Spirito; in the background are the Vatican Gardens and the tower now used by Vatican Radio. Among the buildings at the foot of the hill was an armoury, according to the 1866 Census map. St. Peter's fills the centre of the photograph, and on the right is the Vatican Palace – note the eighteenth century clock on the protruding wing which dates back to the reign of Pius V; the courtyard of S. Damaso and the Palazzo of Sixtus V. The building which would later close off the courtyard on the piazza side has yet to be built (by Filippo Martinucci in 1860). The arcades on the far side of the courtyard have already been filled in with glass.   C.P.

140

ST. PETER'S AND THE PALACE OF THE HOLY OFFICE

(1858 catalogue, no. 59: 'St. Peter's with the Inquisition'; 30.2 × 40.3 cm; private collection.)

The facade and left side of the Vatican basilica. In the foreground is the Palace of the Holy Office, formerly the property of Cardinal Lorenzo Pucci; part of its unadorned facade still survives. The dates 1815, 1843 and 1850 written in chalk on the walls are typical of the way in which Roman builders worked and are very useful in documenting the restoration work done on the building. They may refer to the extensions jutting out beneath them. The palazzo was still unfinished when it was bought by Pius V and converted into the seat of the Holy Office between 1566 and 1572. The facade on to St. Peter's was re-done under Pius IX (1869), while the principal one belongs to the reign of Pius XI (by Ignazio Guidi in 1926). The somewhat severe exterior hides an elegant arcaded central courtyard with a fountain.

C.P.

THE VATICAN PALACE AND COURTYARD OF S. DAMASO

(attributed to Macpherson, about 1854; 37.4 × 27.3 cm; private collection.)

Behind the Bernini fountain (1677) is the Braccio di Costantino (Constantine wing), which is closed by the Portone di Bronzo (Bronze Door); note that its windows are still completely open.

Above it is the building constructed under Paul V, with the elegant Clement XI clock removed in 1860. This photograph is rather unusual because it shows the arcades on the far side of the courtyard of S. Damaso and on the first floor of the wall on the right still without their glass windows. It demonstrates how the addition of the windows has deprived the courtyard of its airy atmosphere and of the dramatic effects of the shadows. The portico built by Martinucci in 1860, which closed off the courtyard at the piazza end with a series of low arcades, is also missing.

C.P.

FOUNTAIN IN THE PIAZZA OF ST. PETER'S

(1858 catalogue, no. 212: 'One of the Vatican fountains in the Piazza of St. Peter's; 28.5 × 39.3 cm; collection of Gianfranco De Santis, Rome.)

In the foreground are the fountain by Maderna (1614) and the colonnade by Bernini. The building under construction behind the statues may be the one designed by Filippo Martinucci in 1860 to close off that side of the S. Damaso courtyard. The picture gives good view of the clock on the wall of the building erected under Paul V, for which Maderna was probably the architect. It has a large face with twelve numerals, and a small bell-tower above it containing three bells. The heraldic signs of the stars and triple-humped hills allude to the pontificate of Clement XI (1700-1721). The subtle way that the face has been inserted into the seventeenth century building is probably the work of Carlo Fontana; there is an inscription under the window below. The clock was removed some time after 1860, when the addition of two clocks designed by Valadier to the facade of St. Peter's made it unnecessary. In 1981 an image of the Virgin Mary in mosaics was set up in its place.

In the background are the arcades of the courtyard of S. Damaso; the upper ones were enclosed by glass during the reign of Gregory XVI (1840-42), and the second (the arcade by Raphael) under Pius IX (1853-54).

C.P.

THE CORTILE DELLA PIGNA

(1858 catalogue, no. 36: 'The Garden in the Vatican styled 'Della Pigna', containing the marble base of a Column dedicated to Antoninus; architecture of Bramante'; 29.2 × 38.4 cm; collection of Christie's, South Kensington, London.)

The Cortile della Pigna (Courtyard of the Fir Cone) has been a garden ever since the reign of Clement XI, and many of the original pots filled with citrus trees and decorated with the Albani coat of arms are still to be found there. The same pope also altered the double flight of steps and placed the great bronze 'Pigna' (which had been in the Vatican since the 1600s) in its present position on top of a capital from the Baths of Severus Alexander. Even the architecture of the niche was changed; the large papal crest is indicative of the extent of the work carried out. A second phase in the development of the courtyard occurred during the reign of Gregory XVI, who in 1835 commissioned the architect Gaspare Salvi to place the base of the Column of Antoninus Pius in the centre. Formerly in the Cortile della Zitella, the base was restored by Giuseppe Fabris and officially opened on 2 February 1846; the balustrade around it was inspired by those which appear on ancient coins featuring the column. The little marble seats in the garden were brought from the Villa Cybo at Castel Gandolfo, having been taken originally by Cardinal Cybo from the Villa della Rinchiostra. Gregory XVI also had four fountains built in the garden, but the one beneath the 'Pigna' is the only one still standing. Note the windows between the pilasters on the second floor of the facade. These had been made quite recently, to illuminate the Etruscan Museum established there in 1836.

C.P.

(1858 catalogue, no. 37: 'Bas-relief
on the base of the Antonine Column,
representing the Apotheosis of
Antoninus and Faustina; in the
garden of the Vatican'; 28.9 × 39.1
cm; private collection.)

On the back of the Column of
Antoninus Pius, opposite the
inscription commemorating
the restoration work done by
Fabris in 1846, is depicted the
Apotheosis of Antoninus and
Faustina, who are being
conducted to heaven by a
winged figure, the *genius* of
Aeternitas (Eternity). Flanked
by symbolic personifications
of Rome and the *Campus
Martius*, the *genius* holds aloft
the obelisk of Augustus, which
is now in the Piazza
Montecitorio. A few features
were actually changed during
the restoration work (for
instance, the fingers on the
right hand of the Goddess of
Rome and the fold of cloth
hanging down from the right
leg of the personification of
the *Campus Martius*,
etc). C.P.

(1858 catalogue, no. 38-39: 'Bas-
relief representing the Funeral
Games, on the other sides of the base
of the Antonine Column';
28.9 × 39.5 cm; private collection.)

On the sides of the Column of
Antoninus Pius (now to be
seen in the Cortile della
Corazza of the Vatican
Museums), are scenes from the
decursio funebris, the games
performed by the Roman
cavalry during the funeral
ceremonies of the emperor and
his wife. Much of this scene
was completed by Fabris
(1846), but some restoration
work had already been carried
out in the eighteenth century
by Vincenzo Felici and
Giuseppe Napolioni.

C.P.

VATICAN MUSEUMS – COLOSSAL HEAD OF AUGUSTUS

(1858 catalogue, no. 65: 'Colossal Head of the Emperor Domitian, the Vatican Musem'; 39.7 × 27.7 cm; private collection. This subject does not appear in the 1863 catalogue; another picture appears under the same number.)

This head, which has since been identified as that of the Deified Augustus, formed part of an enormous acrolith, a seated statue supported on wooden scaffolding, wearing clothes made out of bronze, with all the uncovered parts of the body (head, arms, legs or just feet), added in marble. Since the Renaissance, the sculpture had stood in the exedra of the courtyard, or 'theatre' of the Villa Mattei, near to the Egyptian obelisk from the Capitoline. It remained there until 1801, and in 1802 was bought by the Vatican Museums and placed in the Cortile della Pigna.

C.P.

VATICAN MUSEUMS – THE LAOCOÖN

(1858 catalogue, no. 81: 'The Laocoon; Vatican Museum; 38.4 × 28.9 cm; private collection. The photograph has been slightly cropped on the left side, with the loss of some details.)

It is still not known whether this famous Greek sculpture of the Late Hellenistic period is the original or just a copy. This photograph shows it as it was restored in the sixteenth century; the additional pieces were removed during the scientific restoration project headed by Magi in 1958-60.

It is interesting to note that the hands of the sons of the priest of Apollo have their fingers in slightly different positions when compared to the sculpture as we know it today. It would seem from the photograph that a certain amount of restoration work must have been carried out between 1858 and 1958.

C.P.

VATICAN MUSEUMS SLEEPING ARIADNE

(1858 catalogue, no. 78: 'The Sleeping Ariadne, formerly called the Cleopatra; Hall of the Philosophers, Vatican; 38.6 × 29.7 cm; private collection.)

This famous sculpture, a copy of the original Asiatic masterpiece of the second century B.C., was one of the earliest sculptures to be added to the Vatican collection. Acquired by the reign of Julius II (1503 – 1513), it was used first of all as a fountain in a corner of the octagonal courtyard, and then as a back-cloth in the 'Corridore della Libreria' (Chiaramonti Sculpture Gallery) during the reign of Julius III; later on, under Clement XIV, it was placed on a gigantic sarcophagus beside the entrance to the new Museo Clementino, and it finally ended up in the Gallery of the Statues, which was extended by Simonetti under Pius IV after the demolition of the Mantegna Chapel (in 1780). The setting by Christopher Unterberger has an Egyptian flavour, as in 1780 the figure was still believed to be Cleopatra; it contains a pyramid, a palm tree and an Egyptian statue in armour (hardly visible in the photograph), which is probably Anthony, the Triumvir.

As this decoration no longer survies, the photograph constitutes a precious document of the history of the Vatican Museums.

C.P.

ST. PETER'S AND THE VATICAN PALACE FROM CASTEL
SANT'ANGELO

(atributed to Macpherson, around 1858; 27.9 × 36.8 cm; private collection.)

The view was taken from the Castel Sant'Angelo; in the foreground are clusters
of houses, since demolished, in the Borgo S. Angelo, and the 'Corridore' with
its double roofs resting on the battlements.
To the right, the line of houses along the Borgo Pio reaches the Vatican near the
truncated tower of Nicholas V. St. Peter's and the Vatican Palace form a
dramatic backdrop behind the little houses of the Borgo. Rising up among the
rooftops is the church of S. Maria in Traspontina, one of the few old buildings
to survive the demolition of the Borgo and the creation of the Via della
Conciliazione under Mussolini.

C.P.

THE COUNTRYSIDE
AROUND ROME AND LAZIO

THE CAFFARELLA VALLEY

(1858 catalogue, no. 155: 'Valley of Egeria'; 28.7 × 39.2 cm; Archivio Fotografico Communale., Rome. Donated by Simonetti.)

The vast Caffarella estate is named after the Caffarelli family, but in the nineteenth century it belonged to the Torlonia family, who over the years initiated a number of excavations which have resulted in some important epigraphic and artistic discoveries. The estate is crossed by the 'Marrana della Caffarella', said to be the famous River Almo of antiquity, where the priests of the *Magna Mater* used to come every year on 27 March to wash the image of the goddess. The valley was once a popular place for weekend excursions among the Roman populace, as Peresio tells us in his *Maggio romanesco overo il Palio conquistato*: *"La Caffarella è una villetta a un miglio: Fora de Roma verso Oriente spiana, / Che fanno i Romaneschi un gran bisbiglio, / Le feste 'l maggio intorna a 'na fontana..."*. Macpherson calls it the valley of Egeria, because this is how it was known in ancient times.

P.B.

THE VIA APPIA ANTICA FROM THE BASILICA OF S. SEBASTIANO

(1858 catalogue, no. 46: 'Tomb of Cecilia Metella, and view of the Via Appia, from the Church of St. Sebastian'; 28.1 × 38.2 cm; private collection.)

A classic panorama of the Via Appia Antica taken from the top of the Basilica of S. Sebastiano fuori le Mura. None of the basilica can be seen, as it is to the right of the large piazza on the right of the photograph. On the left is a grey granite column commemorating the restoration of the Via Appia as far as *Bovillae*, carried out under Pius IX in 1852. The completely deserted road is dominated by the round battlemented tomb of Caecilia Metella. Oval versions of this view exist.

P.B.

VIEW OF THE MAUSOLEUM OF ROMULUS AND THE CIRCUS OF MAXENTIUS

(attributed to Macpherson, about 1856; 25.7 × 38 cm; collection of P. Becchetti, Rome.)

Macpherson took another picture of this view some time later, in which the the house of the Torlonia family has a new roof; here it is shown undergoing repairs. The house has been built practically on top of the Mausoleum of Romulus, son of the Emperor Maxentius. Behind the mausoleum is the Circus of Maxentius in all its glory, where the obelisk taken from the *Campus Martius* and now in the Piazza Navona used to stand. But the real splendour of the view lies in the Roman countryside and the long line of aqueducts stretching from Tor Fiscale up to the Alban Hills.

P.B.

THE VIA APPIA ANTICA – TOMB OF CAECILIA METELLA

(1858 catalogue, no. 153: 'Tomb of Cecilia Metella, from the road, 'Via Appia'; 37.1 × 30.1 cm; private collection.)

Constructed towards the end of the Roman Republic as the tomb of the young Caecilia Metella, this structure was converted into a fortress by the Byzantines, on account of its strategic location within sight of the City Walls. In the eleventh century it became the property of the Count of Tusculum, who fortified the tomb; some of this work still survives.
The castle was built by the Caetani family, who acquired the monument at the end of the century; in 1312 it was subjected to a violent siege by the imperial troops of Henry VII, during which it was captured, burned and partially demolished. It continued to decline over the years until all it was fit for was a hide-out for brigands and thieves. The former tomb was in such a bad state that in 1589 it was ordered to be demolished completely, so that the materials could be used elsewhere. Work was already underway when the 'Conservatore' Paolo Lancellotti intervened in the Senate to stop the destruction.

P.B.

THE TOMB OF CAECILIA METELLA, WITH ROME IN THE DISTANCE

(1858 catalogue, no. 45: 'Tomb of Cecilia Metella, with distant view of Rome'; 28.2 × 38.7 cm; private collection.)

This unusual view shows the side of the tomb which looks out over the countryside. The mausoleum is partially covered in the ivy which Byron recalls in his *Childe Harold's Pilgrimage*. The fortifications were built by the Caetani family, who also decorated the entire structure with their Ghibelline coat of arms. The view of Rome and St. Peter's behind comes as quite a surprise; in the centre is the Albani Chapel of the Basilica of S. Sebastiano and on the right, the other ruins of the Circus of Maxentius. Macpherson also produced an oval version of this view.

P.B.

VIEW OF TOMBS ON THE VIA APPIA ANTICA

(1858 catalogue, no. 84: 'View of Tombs on the Via Appia'; 26.2 × 37.6 cm; private collection.)

This view of the only curve on the Via Appia Antica between Rome and Frattocchie makes effective use of a low viewpoint. It also illustrates the strangeness of this stretch of the road, which then resumes its previous course. No doubt Appius Claudius wished to treat this sacred place with particular respect; this was where the ancient sanctuary was built to mark the boundary between Rome and Alba Longa. On the right are the tumuli said to be the tombs of the *Curiatii* and the *Horatii*; the trees which surround them today have not yet been planted. The entire stretch of the road is scattered with fragments of marble which are not to be seen today; they have either been covered up by weeds or stolen.

P.B.

VIEW OF THE CLAUDIAN AQUEDULT

(1858 catalogue, no. 103: 'Large view of the Claudian Aqueduct'; 26.3 × 40.5 cm; collection of P. Becchetti, Rome.)

Much has been written on the splendours of the Roman countryside – of its solitude, its characteristic monuments and its aqueducts, but perhaps Ruskin is the best interpreter of this last aspect of the landscape: 'There is no spectacle on earth that can equal the richness of emotions offered by the Roman countryside... the line of its aqueducts resemble an immense row of weeping willows which dwell on the tomb of an emperor...'

P.B.

ALBANO – THE SO-CALLED TOMB OF ARUNS

(althought it bears Macpherson dry stamp and the number 152, altered to 168, in pencil, this photograph is not included in any of the printed catalogues; about 1860; 5.7 × 17.7 cm; Archivio Fotografico Comunale, Rome.)

Just after leaving Albano and before the large viaduct of Ariccia, a narrow road leads off to the right to the church of S. Maria della Stella. This church is famous for the catacombs of San Senatore and for the impressive tomb in the centre of the picture, commonly knows as the tomb of the *Horatii* and the *Curiatii* or of *Aruns*. In fact, the tomb dates from the last years of the Roman Republic, and it is not known for whom it was built.

P.B.

FRASCATI – SANCTUARY OF THE CHURCH OF THE MADONNA DELLA CONCEZIONE AT CAPOCROCE

(1858 catalogue, no. 107: 'Church of 'Capo-Croce', near Frascati'; not included in the 1871 catalogue; 27.8 × 36 cm; collection of P. Becchetti, Rome.)

The story goes that a country chapel used to stand on this spot, in which there was a fresco of the Madonna and child, known locally as 'The Madonna of Capo Croce'. In 1527, when the soldiers returning from the Sack of Rome stopped here and spared Frascati, the painting was immediately believed to be a worker of miracles. A small shrine was built, and later, as the cult spread, this sanctuary was erected during the reign of Paul V (1615-1621). An adjoining house was added for the Teatini, who were the guardians of the painting until 1910, when it was handed over to the Congregation of the Salesians. In the course of the terrible bombing of Frascati on 29 January 1944, the sanctuary was destroyed. Only the facade was spared, and this was used as part of the new building. Macpherson loved to spend time in his summer house in Frascati; he must have known and loved this solitary spot well to have taken such a sensitive shot of the sanctuary from one side. It may even be that, as a devout Catholic, he intended the photograph more as a tribute to the Madonna than as a record of the rather unremarkable architecture of the church.

P.B.

161

VIEW OF THE PORT OF ANZIO

(1863 catalogue, no. 220: 'Porto d'Anzio, fron the beach near the Villa Aldobrandini'; 24.1 × 40.1 cm; Archivio Fotografico Comunale, Rome.)

Macpherson took two other photographs of the Port of Anzio – this one stretches from the lighthouse right across to the furthest houses of this ancient city (which received a lot of attention during the reign of Pius IX, the 'Restorer of Anzio'). The one numbered 221 shows the beach and the Villa Borghese, while 222 shows the port, the coast and the Villa Borghese. Probably due to the fact that they were not in much demand, these views of Anzio were eliminated from the 1871 catalogue.

P.B.

VIEW OF THE CITY OF NINFA

(1863 catalogue, no. 206: 'The deserted city of Ninfa, in the Pontine Marshes'; 21.5 × 39.9 cm; Archivio Fotografico Comunale, Rome; donated by the Simonetti family.)

In an unforgettable passage in his *Passegiate per l'Italia*, Gregorovius calls Ninfa the 'medieval Pompeii' and remembers the blanket of ivy and flowers that covers the ruins, the towers, the roads and the houses of the deserted city, which must surely, he thinks, be the home of fairies, elves, nymphs and other creatures from the world of fairy tales. He is also impressed by the deep water all around, and by the sublime silence of the place, broken only by the cry of a blackbird roosting in the tower of the old castle.

P.B.

VELLETRI – THE PONTE PIO AT S. ANATOLIA UNDER CONSTRUCTION

(Both these photographs are missing from the 1863 catalogue, where no. 294 is described as a view of the railway bridge under construction: 'The Valley of St. Anatolia, with the New Railway Viaduct'; photo A – 23.2 × 38 cm; photo B – 24.3 × 40 cm; about 1862; collection of the Biblioteca Luigi Poletti, Modena.)

The most impressive achievement of the Rome-Velletri railway line was without doubt the iron bridge across the S. Anatolia valley near Velletri. It was considered one of the most important examples of its kind in Europe. The iron frame rested on four supports – the outer two made of brick and the central two of iron; the central ones featured 'three clearly-defined classical columns – two Doric and one Ionic – which rose up to a height of 41 metres from the valley floor. Iron girders forty-six metres long, constructed according to the Brulow system, were placed on top. The first picture shows the first girder being placed in position; the other documents a later stage in the work.

P.B.

164

VIEW OF THE CITIES OF NORMA AND NORBA

(attributed to Macpherson, about 1860; 26 × 37 cm; collection of P. Becchetti, Rome.)

On the right, on the edge of the precipice, is the medieval city of Norma, first mentioned in the eighth century. In the foreground are the remains of the ancient city of Norba, the Latin city inhabited first by the Volsci and then made a colony of Rome. The city remained loyal to Rome during the Punic Wars, but suffered grave damage during the fighting between Marius and Sulla, and was finally deserted during the years of the Empire. The crumbling ancient terraces, constructed in an effort to even out the ground, add drama to the scene.

P.B.

THE WALLS OF THE ANCIENT CITY OF NORBA

(attributed to Macpherson, about 1860; 24.6 × 37 cm; collection of P. Becchetti, Rome.)

The remarkable ruins of Norba include the acropolis, the city walls in polygonal cyclopean masonry which defended it, and the imposing remains of the Porta Grande, or Great Gate. The shepherd sitting on the left with his dog makes the ruins look even more impressive.

P.B.

PALIANO – VIEW OF THE CASTLE

(attributed to Macpherson, about 1865; 17.5 × 22.1 cm; collection of P. Becchetti, Rome.)

According to the archaeological journalist, playwright and anticlerical writer Edmond About, in his *Roma Contemporanea* of 1860, Paliano had a population of 4,250, with 50 guardsmen, 30 people in prison and 250 political prisoners held in the tower donated to the Papal Government by the Principe Aspreno Colonna on 4 June 1844.

P.B.

THE VIA FLAMINIA – VIEW OF BORGHETTO

(1863 catalogue, no. 171: 'Valley of the Tiber at Ponte Felice, near Borghettaccio, between Civitacastellana and Otricoli'; 31.6 × 40 cm; Archivio Fotografico Comunale, Rome, donated by the Simonetti family.)

Before it reaches the Ponte Felice, the Via Flaminia offers this spectacular view of the Tiber Valley and the Sabine Hills. On the left are the impressive ruins of the castle commonly known as the 'Castellaccio', probably built in the Middle Ages to defend the Tiber landings and the small port of Magliano. The little cluster of houses in the middle is the village of Borghetto, deprecatingly referred to as 'Borghettaccio' in Macpherson's caption; further down the slightly sloping road is the Ponte Felice. Built by Augustus, the bridge was throughly restored by Pope Sixtus V in 1589, and was known from then on as the Ponte Felice, after the pope's baptismal name. It was destroyed during the Second World War. The Tiber was navigable up to this point.

P.B.

NEAR CASTEL MADAMA – VIEW OF THE AQUEDUCTS

(1858 catalogue, no. 124: 'Aqueduct near Castel Madama'; private collection.)

The aqueduct of the *Anio Novus*, like that of the Acqua Claudia, was begun by
Caligula in 38 A.D. and finished under Claudius in the year 52. It originated
near Subiaco and for the most part followed the route of the Acqua Claudia.
The aqueduct was 86,876 m. long and had the greatest capacity of them all –
189,520m^3 of water. It arrived at Rome in the ancient quarter of *ad Spem
Veterem*, where the Porta Maggiore now stands.

C.P.

NEPI – ROCCA DEI BORGIA

(1858 catalogue, no. 170: 'Ruins of the Baronial Stronghold at Nepi, the hunting seat of Lucrezia
Borgia'; 39.9 × 31.7 cm; collection P. Becchetti.)

A splendid view of the 'Rocca dei Borgia' (Castle of the Borgias), one of Nepi's
most important monuments, made even more dramatic by the mill-weel
beneath the gushing water. This mighty construction was erected by Rodrigo
Borgia in 1450, before he became Pope Alexander VI; it was then handed over
to the Farnese family and was later allowed to fall into decay. In addition to its
strong walls, the fortress also had four towers – three cylindrical in shape and
one square one.

P.B.

OSTIA ANTICA – EXCAVATION OF THE 'IMPERIAL PALACE'

(attributed to Macpherson, about 1865; 26 × 38.3 cm; private collection.)

Some photographs of Ostia Antica appear for the first time in Macpherson's 1871 catalogue, as if the monuments of this renowned archaeological centre had not aroused his interest earlier. As this photograph does not bear his stamp, we cannot be certain that he took it. In 1860-61 excavations were carried out in the west side of the ancient city under P.E. Visconti on the orders of the Papal Government. An enormous complex of buildings was discovered which, on account of its rich marble decorations and luxurious furnishings, came to be known as the 'Imperial Palace'; it appears today under this name in the Museo Gregoriano Profano in the Vatican.

A large mosaic was removed to decorate the floor of the Hall of the Immaculate Conception, also in the Vatican. Note the visitors looking around the ruins and the workman in the background with his wheelbarrow, hard at work on the excavations.

P.B.

TIVOLI – THE 'TEMPLE OF VESTA'

(1858 catalogue, no. 116: 'Temple of the Sibyl, seen from the Bridge; 29.8 × 40.6 cm; collection of Martin and Ronchetti.)

Rather than the splendid 'Temple of Vesta', the real subject of this photograph is the dramatic rock-face beneath it. The plants which cling to the sides help to emphasise the carefully-observed play of light and shade between the crags.

P.B.

TIVOLI – ROCCA PIA

(1858 catalogue, no. 123: 'Castle of Tivoli'; 26.8 × 36.6 cm; rectangular photo-collection of P. Becchetti, Rome; oval photo – private collection.)

Macpherson's technical and artistic abilities can be appreciated to the full in this view of the Rocca Pia, the huge symbol of papal power built to overawe the natives of Tivoli. The rectangular and oval versions of the same view are indicative of the two different sides of the author's talent.

P.B.

TIVOLI – PANORAMA OF THE CITY AND THE CASCADES OF THE ANIENE

(1858 catalogue, no. 118: 'Large waterfall, Tivoli'; 29.7 × 39.1 cm; private collection.)

Tivoli has always been popular with visitors to Rome, not only on account of its many ancient monuments, but also for its healthy atmosphere, beautiful countryside and famous villas. Photographers as well as artists helped to spread the word about its great beauty, and Macpherson was among those particularly attracted to the city. He took a great number of interesting photographs there, such as this fantastic panorama of the cascades and the Roman countryside.

P.B.

TIVOLI – LARGE WATERFALL

(1858 catalogue, no. 118: 'Large Waterfall, Tivoli'; 37.5 × 28.4 cm; private collection.)

The waterfall was created when the course of the Aniene was altered during work on the tunnel of Monte Catillo, commissioned by Gregory XVI and officially opened in 1835. The upper part of the tunnel is just visible over the top of the falls.
There is no doubt that the Aniene was probably more picturesque before this work was carried out, but it was very prone to flooding.

P.B.

TIVOLI – CYPRESS TREES IN THE VILLA D'ESTE

(1858 catalogue, no. 121: 'Cypresses in the Villa d'Este, Tivoli'; 38.5 × 28.3 cm; private collection.)

The most striking features of the Villa d'Este are the torrents of water gushing from its many fountains and the lush vegetation. With daring perception, Macpherson chose a group of cypresses to dominate this view and in doing so, has given us one of the most beautiful photographs of his collection.

P.B.

TIVOLI – 'TEMPIO DELLA TOSSE'

(1858 catalogue, no. 120: 'Temple, styled 'Della Tosse', Tivoli'; 29.8 × 40.2 cm; private collection.)

On the ancient Via Tiburtina, before the Porta del Colle in Tivoli and almost opposite the Villa of Maecenas, is this most unusual monument, known as the 'Tempio della Tosse'. It is uncertain how the monument came by this name, but it is now thought to have been built as the mausoleum of the family of M. Turcius Secondus Apronianus, manager of the maintenance works on the Via Tiburtina. The picturesque octagonal structure, topped by a dome, has captured the imagination of many artists, such as Sangallo and Canina. Traces of Byzantine frescoes and decorations suggest that the tomb was at one time adapted for Christian worship.

P.B.

180

TUSCANIA – FACADE OF THE CHURCH OF SANTA MARIA

(1858 catalogue, no. 143: 'Principal Doorway of the above (facade of the Church of Santa Maria, at Toscanella)' 36.4 × 29.7 cm; private collection.)

Macpherson took two photographs of this building: one shows part of the temple and bell tower, while this one focuses on the central entrance. The wide door is flanked by two spirally-fluted columns supported by lions, and in the door jambs are carved figures of the apostles Peter and Paul, guarding the church. Unfortunately the church was vandalised in 1967 and the statue of St. Peter lost its beautiful, noble head.

P.B.

VICOVARO – CHURCH OF S. GIACOMO

(1858 catalogue, no. 52: 'Font of a Gothic Church at Vicovaro, near Tivoli'; 38.9 × 26.7 cm; private collection.)

The graceful octagonal church of S. Giacomo is the most important monument in the town of Vicario. It was begun in the 'Renaissance-Gothic' style in 1454 by Domenico di Capodistria, and the upper part was almost certainly completed by Giovanni Dalmata about ten years later.

P.B.

VITERBO – FOUNTAIN IN THE PIAZZA DELLA ROCCA

(not included in any of Macpherson's catalogues, but attributed to him; about 1860; 27.5 × 38.1 cm; private collection.)

This fountain, which is younger than the others which have made Viterbo famous, was built in 1575 to a design by Raffaele da Montelupo. Almost completely destroyed by bombing during the Second World War, it was quite recently rebuilt using what remained of the original pieces. On the right is the imposing mass of the 'Rocca' (Castle) constructed in 1354 and then rebuilt and decorated under the reigns of Boniface IX, Pius II, Julius II and Paul III. Five crests adorn the entrance gate; the one on the bottom left bears the coat of arms of Pius IX.

P.B.

... BEYOND LAZIO

ORVIETO – VIEW OF THE CITY

(attributed to Macpherson, about 1865; 18 × 22.8 cm; collectionof P. Becchetti, Rome.)

Orvieto is one of the most remarkable cities in Italy. Rising up like an island on a steep-sided plateau of volcanic tufa, it is important both for its spectacular location and for its medieval and Etruscan past. Its most important building is the Duomo on the right of the photograph – a real artistic and architectural masterpiece.

P.B.

ORVIETO – FACADE OF THE DUOMO

(1858 catalogue, no. 130: 'Cathedral of Orvieto'; 32.3 × 27.2 cm; private collection.)

Part of the facade of this famous cathedral is hidden by clumsy wooden structures put up during the restoration of the mosaics.
Above the left hand entrance is a sort of airborne hut with three floors, reached by means of a precarious-looking stairway.

P.B.

ORVIETO – SIDE DOOR OF THE CATHEDRAL

(1858 catalogue, no. 132: 'Side door on the left, with Bas-reliefs'; 27 × 36.7 cm; private collection.)

The four large pilasters between the doors of the Duomo are clad with marble panels depicting stories from the Old and New Testaments and the Acts of the Apostles. The photograph shows the left two pilasters, with stories from the Creation onwards. The figures are very delicately modelled and the scenes show a lively narrative sense.

P.B.

ORVIETO – DETAIL OF FRESCO BY LUCA SIGNORELLI IN THE DUOMO

(1858 catalogue, no. 144: 'Group from a Fresco by Luca Signorelli, at Orvieto'; 24.4 × 29.8 cm; collection of P. Becchetti, Rome.)

Macpherson did not take many photographs of paintings and frescoes. This group by Luca Signorelli in the Duomo at Orvieto is an exception. The long vertical line through the image was made by a crack in the plate.

P.B.

ASSISI – DOORWAY OF THE MIDDLE CHURCH OF THE BASILICA OF ST. FRANCIS

(1858 catalogue, no. 181: 'The Doorway and Portico of the Middle Church or Crypt of San Francesco at Assisi'; 38.8 × 31.2 cm; collection of Sommer, London.)

Goethe may have gone into ecstasies over the Temple of Minerva, but he was not similarly affected by the famous monuments dedicated to St. Francis which were the pride of Assisi and the entire Catholic world. In fact, in his *Italian Journey*, he writes: 'I turned away in distaste from the enormous substructure of the churches on my left, which are built one on top of the other like a Babylonian Tower, and are the resting place of St. Francis. I was afraid that the people gathering inside would all be of the same stamp as my captain'.

P.B.

ASSISI – TEMPLE OF MINERVA

(1863 catalogue, no. 178: 'The Temple of Minerva in the Forum of Assisi'; 41 × 28 cm; collection of P. Becchetti, Rome.)

In his *Italian Journey*, Goethe describes the Temple of Minerva in these words: 'Lo and behold' – there it stood, the first complete classical monument I have seen. A modest temple, just right for such a small town, yet so perfect in design that it would be an ornament anywhere... One could never tire of looking at the facade and admiring the logical procedure of the architect... I cannot describe the sensations which this work aroused in me, but I know they are going to bear fruit for ever'. (October, 1786).

P.B.

PERUGIA – FOUNTAIN IN THE PIAZZA DEL DUOMO

(1858 catalogue, no. 136: 'Fountain in the piazza del Duomo at Perugia'; 27.3 × 39.4 cm; private collection.)

This fountain, known as the 'Maggiore', is one of the glories of Perugia. Designed by Brother Bevignate of Perugia, it was constructed in the second half of the thirteenth century and decorated with sculpture by Nicolò and Giovanni Pisano and probably by Arnolfo di Cambio. Restored and tampered with many times over the centuries, it was carefully restored to its original state in 1950. The statuettes on the upper basin were put back in their proper place and order, and additions like the small group of bronze lions and griffins on the top were removed.

P.B.

PERUGIA – FOUNTAIN IN THE PIAZZA DEL DUOMO

(1858 catalogue, no. 184: 'The fountain of the Pisani at Perugia, looking towards the Duomo'; 28 × 35.8 cm; private collection.)

Under the arch on the left is the Papal Post Office, with its conspicuous crest of Pius IX above the door.

P.B.

PERUGIA – ORATORY OF S. BERNARDINO (FACADE)

(1858 catalogue, no. 137: 'Church of S. Bernardino, Perugia'; 32.5 × 27 cm; collection of P. Becchetti, Rome.)

This much-admired building by Agostino di Duccio, enhanced by the fine reliefs which cover its surface, is shown to its best advantage in this very carefully-observed view. The Oratory was built in honour of S. Bernardino, who often came to Perugia to preach to the people in this piazza.

P.B.

PERUGIA – ETRUSCAN GATEWAY

(1858 catalogue, no. 135: 'Etruscan Gateway at Perugia'; 31 × 26.7 cm; private collection.)

This splendid Etruscan arch of Augustus is one of Perugia's most important monuments. Known by many names – the Porta Tezia, the Porta Vecchia, the Porta Pulcra, etc. – it is typical of those ancient monuments where the work of various centuries is superimposed layer upon layer. Here the Etruscan, Roman, Renaissance and Baroque periods combine to create an altogether fascinating conglomeration.

P.B.

NORCIA – EFFECTS
OF THE EARTHQUAKE
OF 9 DECEMBER 1859

(1863 catalogue, no. 187: 'Palazzo
Communale and Church of St.
Benedict in the Great Square of Norcia,
after the Earthquake'; 22.4 × 39.2 cm;
collection of P. Becchetti, Rome.)

Macpherson took three
photographs of the disastrous
earthquake of 9 December 1859.
The worst-affected place was the
lovely town of Norcia in
Umbria. These pictures are
valuable documents of the grave
damage inflicted on the town's
monuments, but they are the
only photographs of catastrophic
events to appear in
Macpherson's catalogues. The
one in question shows the Town
Hall and church of S. Benedetto
in a state of semi-collapse; the
props intended to prevent
further damage and the neat
piles of debris on the right
suggest that Macpherson arrived
some time after the disaster.

P.B.

196

197

NORCIA – RUINS CREATED BY THE EARTHQUAKE OF 9 DECEMBER, 1859

(1858 catalogue, no. 185: 'Street view in Norcia, after the Earthquake, from the Casa Cipriani; 31.1 x 36.7 cm; Biblioteca Luigi Poletti, Modena.)

As Macpherson states in his catalogue, the photograph was taken from the 'Casa Cipriani'. While the *Edicola*, an unusual little travertine structure by Vanni Tuzzi (1354) seems to have survived intact in the foreground, all the buildings on the left side of the road have been damaged, as can be seen from the piles of debris around them.

P.B.

SPOLETO – CHURCH OF SAN PIETRO

(1858 catalogue, no. 273: 'Church of San Pietro fra-i-Monti, at Spoleto'; 37.4 × 27.4 cm; collection of p. Becchetti, Rome.)

The church of S. Pietro was built in a clearing at the foot of the Monteluco at the beginning of the fifth century, by Bishop Achilles, who had brought a relic from the chains of St. Peter back from Rome. Enlarged and reconstructed many times, the church's facade is in the 'Umbrian' style of the twelfth century. The sculptures, by many different hands, are one of the masterpieces of the Middle Ages in Umbria.

P.B.

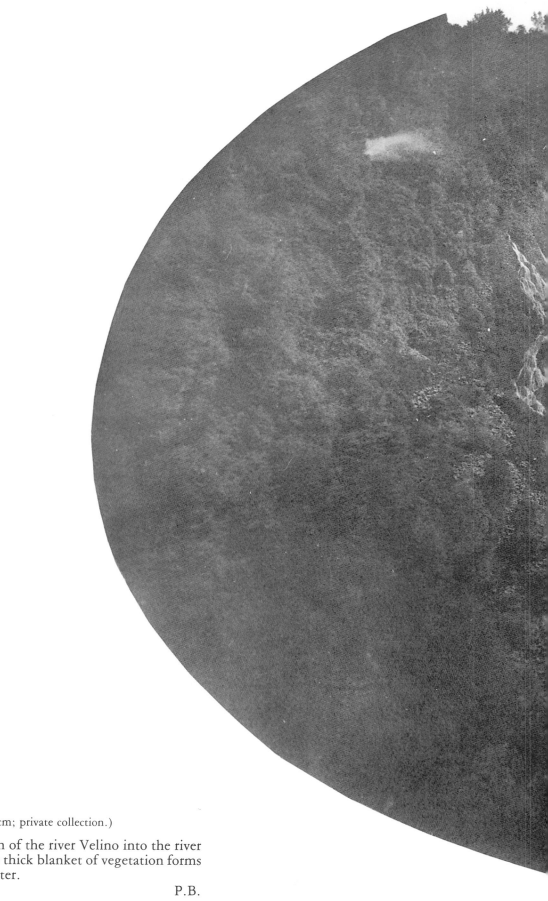

TERNI – THE FALLS OF MARMORE

(1858 catalogue, no. 139: 'Falls of Terni'; 25.3 × 38.2 cm; private collection.)

The Falls of Marmore, created by the diversion of the river Velino into the river Nera, are seen here in all their splendour. The thick blanket of vegetation forms a rich backdrop to the gushing torrents of water.

P.B.

INDEX OF PLACES AND NAMES

INDEX OF PLATES

Printed in April 1988
at the Tipolitografia Amadeus I.P.E., Ariccia
Setting by CSF, Roma
Photo-lithographic reproductions by Art
Color Offset, G. Bartolini, Roma